D R. ADAMS gives a spirited, personal account of his allegiance to one of the most interesting religious groups in the U.S.A. In fact, the Disciples of Christ may claim to be the largest purely indigenous American religious group. They have nearly two million adult communicants and some 8,000 congregations, more or less independent.

The Disciples are often described as a movement. A movement back to the New Testament and a movement forward to ecumenical Christianity. Dr. Adams describes this double movement, and illuminates the ecumenical tendency in all Protestant churches today.

How did the Disciples of Christ begin? As shown by Dr. Adams, two great currents of religious thought came together in the early nineteenth century in the Mid-West. One was called the Christian Church under the leadership of Barton W. Stone; the other was called the Disciples of Christ under the leadership of Thomas Campbell and his son. In 1832 there was a union of the Christian Church and the Disciples of Christ. The antecedents of the leaders of the movement were Presbyterian, and elders play an important role in the church organization of the Disciples.

Important chapters deal with "believer's baptism," and the Communion of the Lord's Supper. The Disciples baptize only those who are adult enough to understand the rite of bap-

(cont'd on back flap)

(cont'd from front flap)

tism, and they baptize by immersion. Communion Service is never omitted. The Disciples admit to the Lord's Supper any baptized person from any sectarian group.

At the conclusion of the account of what the Disciples of Christ believe and what their social concerns are, Dr. Adams paints the goal of the United Church of Christ. He then explains why he remains a Disciple until the great ecumenical day dawns.

ALREADY PUBLISHED "WHY I AM" BOOKS

WHY I AM A METHODIST ..... *Roy L. Smith*

WHY I AM A LUTHERAN ..... *Victor E. Beck*

WHY I AM A PRESBYTERIAN
Park Hays Miller

WHY I AM A BAPTIST ...*Louie D. Newton*

Each, $2.75

Thomas Nelson & Sons
NEW YORK

WHY I AM

A DISCIPLE OF CHRIST

By HAMPTON ADAMS

WHY I AM
A DISCIPLE OF CHRIST

By

Hampton Adams

THOMAS NELSON & SONS

EDINBURGH   NEW YORK   TORONTO

Library of Congress Catalog Card No.: 57-11894

Grateful acknowledgment is made to The Bethany
Press for permission to use several quotations from
The Disciples of Christ by W. E. Garrison and A. T.
DeGroot.

To

JOHN ADAMS

PREFACE

THE TITLE of this book was given by the publishers.
There is a measure of safety for the writer in this phrasing of the subject since he could not presume to speak for the almost two million members of the Christian Church (Disciples of Christ). No individual member of the church could do that.

Because the Disciples of Christ do not have a creed and since their congregational type of church government does not permit any authoritative convention or council to govern the local church, there are sharply divergent opinions and practices within the larger fellowship. Therefore, the writer of this book, perhaps more than the author of any other book in the series on "Why I Am . . .", feels that he must write as an individual minister rather than as a representative of his church.

The title indicates that this is not to be a history of the Disciples of Christ. Had the publishers asked for this, the writer could not have accepted the assignment because

7

Professors Winfred E. Garrison and Alfred T. DeGroot have
written within recent years a comprehensive history of this
church to which the writer who is not a church historian,
could not add anything of importance.

It is at the publisher's request that an autobiographical
strand is to be woven into all the books in this series on the
major denominations.

This book would, of course, be more convincing if it were
written by a person who, after a long search, had found his
spiritual home with the Disciples of Christ. I became a member of this church when I was a child, and the story of the
Disciples as related in these chapters had little to do with
my decision.

Although this attempt to interpret the Disciples of Christ
for the readers is ex post facto reasoning as to Why I Am A
Disciple, I must admit that the restudy that was required by
the assignment gave me enthusiasm for the final chapter on
"Why I Remain a Disciple Until . . ."

I thank my secretary, Mrs. Carl Beeman, for the care that
she has given to the review and typing of the manuscript.

Both Mrs. Adams and I express our gratitude to George
and Polly Wiles who opened their lovely Cape Cod home to
us for a rest-work vacation in which the first draft of this
book was made.

HAMPTON ADAMS

New York City
April 1957

CONTENTS

CONTENTS

WHY I AM

A DISCIPLE OF CHRIST

ONE

MORE OR LESS PERSONAL

I SUPPOSE the first reason that I am a Disciple of Christ is that my mother and her family for several generations back were identified with this peculiarly American religious movement. They lived in Kentucky where the two main forces of the movement consolidated and moved forward with vigor in the early nineteenth century.

However, I cannot say, as some can, that I am a Disciple because my parents before me were Disciples, since my father belonged to another and older denomination. He was a deacon in his church for nearly all of his adult life, and he served his denomination in a number of ways. My father was one of the most earnest Christians I have ever known. I attended Sunday School with him until I united with my mother's church.

An over-zealous evangelist who was conducting a "protracted meeting" in my father's church precipitated my joining my mother's church. On a Saturday night after a week of preaching services in which the response in additions to the church was disappointing, the evangelist evidently made up his mind not to pronounce the benediction until one or more persons joined the church. During the singing of the invitation hymn he went up and down the aisle buttonholing and speaking to persons individually about "giving yourself to Christ." He took hold of my lapel, and above the singing, exhorted me to come out and take my "stand for the Lord." I suppose that at most he did not linger there embarrassing me for more than a minute or two but it seemed like a much longer time. However, I did not leave my position until the service was dismissed. And then on the next day I went with my mother and united with her church. Perhaps if an evangelist in her church had reached me first I would have shown my resentment by joining my father's church.

The decision to go into the church of one parent rather than the other, even under these circumstances, was not easy. Before this impulsive act as an adolescent I had been disturbed by the thought that some day I would have to make this decision. It did not seem right to me that I should have to make it. After all of these years it does not seem right.

Sooner or later I think I might have found my way into the church of the Disciples even though I had united with my father's church first, because the Disciples of Christ have had as their historic mission the uniting of the church of Jesus Christ. I have never been able to consider this mission without deep emotion that traces back to my own divided home where two consecrated parents, because of their different traditions, made their way to separate churches every Sunday. Each loved the other and each respected the Christian convictions of the other but inherited denominational loyalty made it impossible for either to give up his church and unite with the other so that the family might worship together.

I do not remember making a decision to be a minister of the Gospel. Certainly my intention to prepare myself for the ministry antedates my uniting with the church of the Disciples. It seems to me that from my earliest memory I knew that I would be a minister. Whether I would be a preacher in my father's church or my mother's church, was not clear. I often played at being a preacher and since both my mother's church and my father's church practiced immersion, I played at baptizing my little cousins and other playmates. Once I actually immersed another child in a pond on my grandfather's farm. In this instance my father supplemented the sacrament of baptism with the sacrament of the switch.

By the time I graduated from high school I had fully and eagerly determined to attend historic Transylvania College, one of the renowned colleges of the Disciples of Christ. Transylvania is the oldest college west of the Allegheny Mountains. George Washington and Thomas Jefferson made gifts to it. Both the Episcopal and Presbyterian churches had a part in the early history of the college before it became a Disciple institution. Situated in the cultural center of Lexington, Kentucky, Transylvania in the early decades of the twentieth century met head-on the fundamentalism that was agitated by the theories of Darwin and the Biblical and theological liberalism of the time.

On the campus of Transylvania, though not organically connected with it, was one of the foremost seminaries of the Disciples of Christ, the College of the Bible. The leading professors of this seminary had been trained at the University of Chicago and other first rate universities, and found themselves under suspicion by fundamentalist colleagues in the faculty and fundamentalist preachers and church editors in the Disciples fellowship across the nation. Consequently, the funda-

mentalist-modernist controversy as it related to the Disciples
of Christ had its most violent explosion on the Transylvania
campus. For the most part the students in the college and
seminary sided with the younger and more able faculty members who were exponents of liberalism.

Our generation of college and seminary students have carried through our lives both the benefits and the scars of that
controversy. The benefits are those that came to all students
and scholars who were liberated from a literalistic, mechanical
and false view of the Bible by the spirit and tools of the liberal
movement. The new interest in theology and the new ortho-
doxy itself would not have been possible had it not been for
the critical scholarly research in Biblical studies by liberal
scholars.

However, scars of the controversy were burned deep. Before
students could understand the real reasons for the controversy
they allied themselves with their favorite professors and developed an animus toward those of the other school. Furthermore the spirit of devotion and the art of true worship were
all but sacrificed in the acrimonious debate. Liberalism itself
that freed the minds from ancient superstitions and tabus became identified with humanism; and theology was given up
for philosophies of religion and truth that could be scien-
tifically determined. Religion was diluted into moralism and
since morality without religious roots soon withers and dies,
the ethical life itself has suffered from that phase of modern
church history.

Students in Disciple colleges and liberal Disciple seminaries were freer than students in some other denominational
institutions to go to all the extremes allowed by liberalism
because the checks of historic creeds and ecclesiastical authori-
ties were lacking. I would still be willing to face the con-

troversy and accept its scars if there were no other way of escaping the bondage of the fundamentalism of those years. However, a frank evaluation of that experience as a college and seminary student of more than thirty years ago, makes me see that it was not the most fortunate of all times for a young man in the tradition of the Disciples of Christ to get his start in the Christian ministry.

My experience in interdenominational fellowship and the ecumenical movement have increased now through many years my appreciation for the Disciples of Christ. Disciples are very comfortable in the wider fellowship. After taking my Bachelor of Divinity degree at the College of the Bible in Lexington, I earned the degree of Master of Arts at Yale University, having all my classes in Yale Divinity School. Day after day, I attended classes with other young men in training for the ministry without ever inquiring or finding out what denominational connections they had. Although I came to know the denominational affiliations of all my professors it never mattered. Yale had passed beyond the fundamentalist-modernist controversy and it was good to be free from the tensions that lingered in Lexington.

Upon graduating from Yale I returned to Kentucky to a Disciples pastorate. In my second year of that pastorate I was given a three-months' leave of absence to travel in Europe, and at the close of that extended tour I attended in Stockholm, Sweden, the ecumenical conference of "Life and Work," an experience that committed me to the ecumenical movement and convinced me that the historic witness of the Disciples of Christ for the unity of the church would be binding upon my whole ministry.

I was only twenty-eight years old at the time I was accepted as a delegate to the Stockholm Conference because of the

gracious activity in my behalf of the late Peter Ainslie of
Baltimore who for years was the Disciple Voice for Christian
unity. I regret to say that Dr. Ainslie was *persona non grata*
to many of his Disciples brethren because they felt that the
Disciples of Christ would fulfill their mission for Christian
unity by calling all Christians back to the New Testament
church which they thought the Disciples had restored.

In this view of the Disciples of Christ as the only true
church of our Lord these brethren of ours had cancelled
out their own witness for Christian unity. Dr. Ainslie was a
prophet who, while not without honor in his own brotherhood, found himself more at home in interdenominational
fellowship than at the conventions of his own people.

As we shall bring out in the chapters that are to follow,
the Disciples from the beginning of their history have held
in tension their two major objectives: the desire to witness
for the unity of the church; and the restoration of the New
Testament church which many persons in the movement felt
had already been approximated. But those who have insisted
that the Disciples alone have given to the modern world the
true church of Jesus Christ have not had much influence in
restoring the unity of the church.

The Stockholm Conference on Life and Work was a gathering of some fifty denominations and confessions from all over
the world. Meeting within the decade following the First
World War, they showed that their deepest concern was
to realize the unity of the church in Jesus Christ that they
together as The Church—the Universal Church of our Lord—
would be able to prevent a Second World War. In the deepest
humility they confessed their guilt for not being able to prevent the holocaust of the First World War. There was something so moving, so dynamic, so liberating in this gathering

of Christians from many denominations that one felt that he could never again be fenced in by his own denomination. From that time the ecumenical movement has been a prime interest of this writer. From Stockholm I came back to my county seat parish in south central Kentucky to preach again and again on the prayer of our Lord, found in the seventeenth chapter of John's Gospel, "Father, that they may all be one; even as thou, Father, are in me, and I in thee, that they also may be in us, so that the world may believe that thou hast sent me."

I have tried in the communities where I have served, to associate myself with my Christian brethren of all denominations. I have found in doing that that I have not had to move outside of the Disciple tradition but have been within the spirit and mission of my denomination.

It was my privilege to represent the Disciples of Christ at Oxford, England, in the Conference on Life and Work and in Edinburgh, Scotland, in the Conference on Faith and Order in the summer of 1937. Then in 1948 I was an alternate delegate of my church to the First Assembly of the World Council of Churches. In 1954 I was honored by being the chairman of the Disciple delegation at the Second Assembly of the World Council of Churches at Evanston, Illinois.

For a number of years I have been the president of the Disciples' Council on Christian Unity, formerly the Association for the Promotion of Christian Unity. In that organization which was founded by the late Peter Ainslie, I have been involved year after year in the Disciples' planning and strategy on matters relating to Christian unity.

When I think of why I am a Disciple I think primarily of the rapport which Disciples feel when they are in fellowship with their brethren of other denominations.

In addition to having a part in these world assemblies of the church I have had the satisfaction for more than twenty years of being a member of the executive boards, first, of the Federal Council of the Churches of Christ in America and, now, the National Council of the Churches of Christ in the U. S. A.

My satisfaction in this association and in the work having to do with Christian unity has been dimmed many times by the contradictions within my own brotherhood. The Disciples of Christ have by their own actions and especially by their divisions, repudiated many times their witness to the unity of the church. There will be more about this in the main chapters of the book; but, having said this, I must also say that I know of no other denomination that has kept itself so continuously under the judgment of Christ's prayer for the unity of the church and has considered its own divisions as sin, as has the church of the Disciples of Christ. And yet—I suppose this is the paradox of the Disciples of Christ—while I am happy to be a Disciple, I pray for that day when there will be no separate body of Christians known as Disciples of Christ, the day when the unity for which Christ Himself prayed will be realized.

There are other matters about which I might speak in this, now all too personal, introduction. I find freedom that I like in the congregational government of my church, although I do not defend congregationalism as the New Testament pattern of organization because I see in the New Testament the seeds of the Presbyterian and Episcopal forms of church government. Furthermore, I have experienced the extravagance and even anarchism of extreme local church autonomy.

I shall be saying much more about the meaning of the weekly observance of the Lord's Supper in Disciple churches, which I miss when I worship in other churches. And while I am not in favor with all my brethren of the Disciples of Christ because the church that I serve admits to membership unimmersed Christians, yet I want to bear witness to the beauty and symbolic meaning of baptism by immersion. And even more, I want to advocate as we proceed in our story the consideration by all Christian people of the importance of believers' baptism.

From this point on there will be much less of the writer and more of the people known as the Disciples of Christ.

TWO

WHAT IS IN A NAME?

T HERE IS A great deal of confusion about the name, or names, of the brotherhood that is referred to here as the Disciples of Christ. Where our church is best known the designation, Disciple of Christ, is not familiar. The movement that resulted in this peculiarly American church gained its initial strength in Kentucky, Pennsylvania, West Virginia and Ohio and then moved west and south with the migrations of the nineteenth century. In county-seat towns, villages, countryside and cities in the Middle West, South and Northwest our churches are now found among the three or four strongest churches in the community; and on the cornerstone or over the door usually there is the simple name, Christian Church.

The sole use of the word Christian to designate this communion and its individual churches has seemed presumptuous and almost arrogant to many Christians in other denominations. This is unfortunate and foreign to the spirit of most of our churches and the great majority of our people who have never thought of other churches as less Christian than ours or other disciples of our Lord as less Christian than we.

It was in an effort to overcome the sectarian spirit that the name Christian was chosen in the hope—it has proved to be a vain hope—that this name would disassociate our people from sectarianism. However, Alexander Campbell, the most influential of the founding fathers in everything but the selection of the name, was never convinced that the designating of the church as the Christian Church was wise. Campbell always preferred the name, Disciples of Christ, because disciple is an humble word, meaning learner, learner at the feet of the Great Teacher.

The church of which we write was not alone in choosing as its only designation the name "Christian," nor was it the first. A group of people who seceded from the Methodist Church in Virginia and North Carolina in 1794 and formed a separate fellowship, adopted the name, "Christian Church."

In the early years of the eighteenth century there were organized in New England several independent "Christian Churches." In September 1801 an independent church was organized in Linden, Vermont, and given the name "Christian Church." Then there was another Christian Church which was "gathered" in Portsmouth, New Hampshire, on the last Wednesday in March 1803. Garrison and DeGroot state on the authority of an early nineteenth-century journal that there were in 1807 fourteen churches that were called simply "Christian Churches." Again these historians quote correspondence published in 1827 that referred to "nearly 100 companies of free brethren that meet together to worship God in the name of Christ without the addition of any other name." This correspondent, evidently one of the free churchmen, added: "We mean to be New Testament Christians without any sectarian name connected with it, without any sectarian creeds, articles, or confessions, or discipline to eliminate the scripture . . . It is our design to remain free from all human laws, confederations, and unscriptural combinations; and to stand fast in the liberty wherewith Christ has made us free."

The purpose behind these independent movements appears quite clearly to have been the earnest desire of these Christians to disentangle themselves from the denominational factionalism that had reached scandalous proportions at the time. The rigidity of creedal statements as they applied in some churches, caused these "Christians" to deny creedal authority. Instead, they based their belief in the New Testament as they believed themselves capable of interpreting it.

Furthermore, they determined to rid themselves and their local churches from the domination of ecclesiastical authority. Each congregation remained an autonomous church, declaring itself to be independent of any Episcopal, Presbyterian or other higher authority.

As Arthur Schlesinger, Jr., said in his address, "The Age of Alexander Campbell" at the Founders' Day celebration at Bethany College on March 1, 1956, "Democratizing forces, accumulating in the course of the eighteenth century, released during the War of Independence, renewed by the excitements of the election of 1800, and by the pull of Westward expansion, were giving the nation new expectations and new values. Nor could anything hope to escape the democratizing process—not politics, nor literature, nor even religion itself."

The "Christian" movement that had the most direct bearing on the Disciples of Christ was the one in which Barton W. Stone was the leading figure. Stone had been a Presbyterian, but with four other Presbyterian ministers he withdrew from his presbytery in Kentucky and formed another that was independent of the synod. Within a few months, less than ten, they dissolved this presbytery and Stone became the leader of a "Christian" movement. The motives were the same as those that brought about the "Christian" churches in New England.

In the second decade of the nineteenth century Alexander Campbell and Barton W. Stone met for the first time. This meeting resulted in further communications that were climaxed by the merger of the two movements in 1832. Both leaders were opposed to any sectarian designation of the new movement. Barton Stone and his followers preferred the name "Christian" and insisted that it was divinely appointed, giving as their authority the statement in Acts 11:26—"The disciples were called Christian first at Antioch." Campbell, as we have stated, argued for the name "Disciples of Christ."

Throughout our brotherhood in local churches the name "Christian Church" has prevailed although in the religious census we have been listed as "Disciples of Christ" and in almost any listing of major denominations such as that of the National and World Councils of Churches, we are designated by this term.

However, we have never been able to lay full claim to the title "Christian Church" because some of the churches of the Stone movement did not go along with the merger of 1832 and they continued to designate themselves, corporately, as the "Christian Church."

This "Christian Church" kept its identity for almost a full one hundred years, and then in 1931 united with the Congregational Church forming the Congregational-Christian Church. Now within a few months, after years of negotiations, the Congregational-Christian Church and the Evangelical-

Reformed Church are about to consummate a union that will be known as the United Church of Christ in America.

While most of the discussion of the name of our church has been about the preference for either "Christian Church" or "Disciples of Christ," the movement has been subjected to other designations, especially in the earlier years. In derision by some people with a sectarian bias, we were called "Campbellites." For a time we were commonly called "Reformers" and our leaders did not object to the movement's designation as the "Reformation of the Nineteenth Century." Because our churches called for "a return to New Testament Christianity" we did not disclaim the title, "Restoration Movement." But those terms now are seldom heard.

When I began writing this book in the summer of 1956 I would have said that our people are settling more and more on the name of "Disciples of Christ." Now I am not sure. At the International Convention of the Disciples of Christ in Des Moines, Iowa, September 28-October 3, 1956, the assembly manifesting a strong preference for the name "Christian Church," voted to change the name of the convention to "International Convention of the Christian Church (Disciples of Christ)."

THREE

A BIT OF HISTORY

THIS BRIEF SKETCH of the beginnings and development of this American Christian movement is offered with the hope that it will help those who have not hitherto been acquainted with it to understand its place in present-day Protestantism.

Thomas Campbell had no idea of founding a new church when he, for health reasons, migrated from Ireland to western Pennsylvania in 1807. Campbell, of Scotch descent, was born in Ireland in 1763. His father left the Roman Catholic Church to become a member of the Anglican Church. In his young manhood Thomas Campbell belonged to the Anglican Church but he early united with the Presbyterian Church.

At the time, the Presbyterian Church of Scotland was divided into four distinct and separate bodies. There was the main parent body and a division known as the "Seceders" who had withdrawn from it after the Church of Scotland in 1712 had sought to deprive local churches of the right to select their own minister.

27

Within the Seceder Church a sharp question arose as to whether those who had violated the law of the State Church, thereby violating the law of the State, could in good conscience take a civil oath which bound them to support "the religion presently professed within the realm." Some felt that even though they had withdrawn from the State Church they could take this civil oath, and they designated themselves as "Burghers." However, in 1747 a group of Seceders declared that they could not in good conscience take the civil oath and they broke off from the Burghers and called themselves "Anti-Burghers."

Thomas Campbell belonged to the Anti-Burgher brand of the Seceder division of the Presbyterian Church of Scotland. Deplorable as these divisions were, they had meaning in Scotland. But when Thomas Campbell arrived in the United States where Church and State were separated he found the divisions of the Presbyterian Church of Scotland persisting in this land where they had no relevance.

Campbell was a thoughtful, even a scholarly, man and this divided condition of his own Presbyterian Church in America when he arrived in 1807 awakened his mind to what a later Disciple was to call the "scandal of the church." But even when he was still in Ireland, Campbell had tried to overcome the divisions that were in the Scottish Church.

The Synod of his branch of the Presbyterian Church was in session in May 1807 when Campbell landed in Philadelphia. The Synod received him and commended him to the Chartiers Presbytery in the western part of Pennsylvania. This synod represented all of the Seceder Presbyterians in the United States, but in reality it was Anti-Burgher because the Burghers had not organized a church here.

Mr. Campbell soon found himself in difficulties with his

presbytery. Charges were first brought against him on October
27, 1807; and on January 6, 1808 a committee of four persons
filed charges, under seven heads, against him.

The charges were that he, Thomas Campbell: 1) denies
"that any assurance or confidence that we in particular
through the grace of our Lord Jesus Christ shall be saved, belongs to the nature of saving faith"; 2) says that the church has
no divine warrant for holding confessions of faith as terms of
communion; 3) says that it is the duty of ruling elders
(laymen) to pray and exhort publicly in vacant congregations
(i.e., when no minister is present or available); 4) says that it
is "warrantable for the people of our communion to hear
ministers that are in stated opposition to our testimony";
5) asserts "that our Lord Jesus Christ was not subject to the
precept as well as the penalty of the Law in the stead of his
people, or as their surety"; 6) asserts that man "is able in this
life to live without sin in thought, word and deed"; 7) has
preached without regular call or appointment "within the
bounds of the Associate Congregations of Chartiers where the
Reverend Mr. Ramsay is settled."

On February 12 at the end of a four-day meeting of the
Presbytery Mr. Campbell was suspended. He appealed his
case to the Associate Synod of North America which was the
highest court of the Seceder Presbyterians. On May 24 the
Synod revoked the sentence of suspension against Mr. Campbell and resolved to conduct its own trial and consider charges
and answers.

On May 25 this committee made its report and dropped
the last three of the seven charges. On the first four the sub-
stance of the report was: 1) on the charge of teaching that a
sense of assurance is not of the essence of faith—proven guilty
as charged; 2) as to creeds and confessions, Mr. Campbell

seems opposed to the practice of the church. He has taught
publicly that "an agreement of what is expressly taught and
enjoined in the New Testament, either in expressed words or
by proven precedent, should be deemed sufficient in point of
unity and uniformity, and that nothing should be made a
term of communion in the Christian Church which is not as
old as the New Testament, or that is not expressly revealed
and enjoined therein"; 3) on the duties of lay elders, if he
means that ruling elders should exhort, "his encouraging
such a practice" is inconsistent with preserving the Scripture
distinction between the duties of teaching and ruling elders";
4) on occasional hearing, "it is altogether unwarrantable for
a minister belonging to this Synod to advise his hearers to
attend the public administration of those of different communions; the propriety of doing which, however, Mr. Campbell, in his speeches in Synod, has plainly avowed." Summary:
"Upon the whole, the committee are of the opinion that Mr.
Campbell's answers to the first two articles of charge, especially, are so evasive, unsatisfactory and highly equivocal
upon great and important articles of revealed religion as to
give ground to conclude that he has expressed sentiments very
different upon these articles from the sentiments held and professed by this Church, and are sufficient ground for censure."

This committee's report was approved. The next day a
motion to "rebuke and admonish" Mr. Campbell was carried.
After he had been rebuked and admonished the Synod gave
him preaching appointments for two months in its central
city and then lifted the suspension and allowed him to return
to his own Presbytery.

But when he returned to his own Presbytery he found that
there was no disposition to make further appointments for
him. The following September Mr. Campbell declined the

authority of the Presbytery. The Presbytery then voted his suspension and so notified the Synod at its next meeting.

For the year Mr. Campbell continued to preach wherever he could receive a hearing, mostly in the vicinity of Washington, Pennsylvania. He did not attempt to organize a church but as Garrison and DeGroot say, "It may safely be conjectured that his preaching laid emphasis upon those points which had caused the separation—the importance of moving from sectarian divisions to the unity of Christians; the right of direct appeal to Scriptures instead of regarding any church's 'Confession and Testimony' as a standard which no one could question; the consequent rejection of all creeds as a test of fellowship; sole reliance upon 'what is expressly taught and enjoined in the New Testament' as a bond of unity for Christians; a reasonable view of the nature of faith; a demand for freedom for ministers and laymen, as against the conventional restrictions imposed in the interest of clerical prestige and ecclesiastical usage."

Nine months before the final action of the Presbytery expelling Mr. Campbell from the Seceder Presbyterian ministry, a group of his followers, meeting in a private home near Washington, Pennsylvania, resolved to form a society "to give more definiteness to the movement in which they had thus far been cooperating without any formal organization or arrangement."

On August 17, 1809, as a result of this action, the "Christian Association of Washington" was organized, using as its slogan, "Where the Scriptures speak, we speak; where the Scriptures are silent, we are silent." There was no intention of making this Association into a church. Its purpose was to work for reform within the churches.

Thomas Campbell then set to work to write the document

which the Disciples of Christ have always considered to be their Magna Charta. In this ecumenical age many students and scholars of other denominations have come to appreciate it as one of the great historical documents of Protestantism. This document is in two parts: one, a "Declaration," the other, an "Address." It is known as the "Declaration and Address." It was approved by the Christian Association of Washington on September 7, 1809.

Looking back almost one hundred and fifty years on the formulation of "Declaration and Address" we may well conclude that the premise upon which it was written was greatly over-simplified. Garrison and DeGroot have seen in the "Declaration and Address" one basic assumption: namely, "that it is possible to define a simple evangelical Christianity, with a definite body of doctrine and a definite program of ordinances, worship and government for the church, all infallibly derived from the infallible Scriptures and completely uncontaminated by 'human opinion'."

However we need to see this emphasis as the swing of the pendulum from the creedal and theological systems which in that time stood between plain men and the New Testament itself. It was naive, of course, for Campbell and his associates to think that their interpretation of Scripture would be free from human opinion.

It is to be noted in the Declaration it is categorically stated "that this society by no means considers itself a church..." The spirit of the society is revealed in this statement: "This society, formed for the sole purpose of promoting simple, evangelical Christianity, shall to the utmost of its power, countenance and support such ministers and such only as exhibit a manifest conformity to the original standard in conversation and doctrine, in zeal and diligence; only such as reduce to practice that simple form of Christianity expressly exhibited upon the Sacred Page: without attempting to inculcate anything of human authority, or private opinion, or inventions of men, as having any place in the constitution, faith or worship of the Christian Church, or anything as a matter of Christian faith or duty for which there cannot be expressly produced a 'Thus sayeth the Lord,' either in expressed terms or by approval precedent." The Association declared that it would meet twice a year. This was an indication, if further evidence is needed, that it did not intend to become a church.

The Declaration insisted on every man's right to interpret the Scripture for himself; declared that the essential unity of the church provides a recognition of this right; and proclaimed that the pattern of the church is to be found in the New Testament.

Garrison and DeGroot have condensed the thirteen propositions in the "Address" that followed the "Declaration." In this brief resume we feel that we are justified in further reducing these statements.

1. The Church of Christ on earth is essentially, intentionally and constitutionally one.

2. Congregations ought to be in close fellowship with one another though they are necessarily separate and often distant in location.

3. Nothing ought to be an article of faith, a term of communion, or an obligatory rule for the constitution and government of the church except what is expressly taught by Christ and his apostles.

4. The New Testament is as perfect a constitution for the worship, discipline and government of the New Testament church, and as perfect a rule for the particular duties of

its members as the Old Testament was for the Old Testament church.

5. No human authority can make new laws for the church where the Scriptures are silent.

6. Inferences and deductions from Scripture may be true doctrine, but they are not binding upon the consciences of Christians further than they perceive them to be so.

7. Doctrinal exhibitions of the great system of divine truths are highly expedient but must not be made terms of communion, because they are products of human reasoning.

8. Full knowledge of all revealed truth is not necessary to entitle persons to membership in the church, "neither should they, for this purpose, be required to make a profession more extensive than their knowledge." Realization of their need of salvation, faith in Christ as Savior, and obedience to him are all that is essential.

9. All who are thus qualified should love each other as brothers and be united as children of one family.

10. "Divisions among Christians is a horrid evil, fraught with many evils."

11. Divisions have been caused in some cases by neglect of the expressly revealed will of God; in others, by assumed authority to make human opinions the test of fellowship.

12. All that is needed for the purity and perfection of the church is that it receive those, and only those, who profess faith in Christ and obey him according to the Scriptures.

13. When the church is forced to adopt "expedients" in order to observe the divine ordinances, where the necessary means are not revealed, they should be recognized as what they are and should not be mistaken for divine commands.

In the appendix of the "Address," care was given—and this was the main reason for the appendix—to assure members of other churches that it was not the purpose of the Christian Association of Washington to draw away their members. It was stated too, in this appendix, that the Association was not to be considered "latitudinarian" because it had no creed. It was argued that loyalty to Christ and adherence to the New Testament are a sufficient warrant of a sound and saving faith.

About the time the proof sheets of the "Declaration and Address" came from the printer in the autumn of 1809 Alexander Campbell, son of Thomas, came to this country with the other members of his father's family. He had been studying in the University of Glasgow. He had been associated in Glasgow with churchmen and scholars who were concerned to bring about a religious reformation that would give greater independence to local congregations and grant to laymen the right to take responsibility along with ministers for the teaching and guidance of the church.

Furthermore, under the influence of the philosophy of John Locke, these men insisted that man's reason is capable of weighing Scriptural evidence and thereby bringing him to a saving faith. It is not surprising therefore, that when Alexander Campbell read the "Declaration and Address" from the proof sheets he found himself in accord with the position his father had taken, and ready and eager to be associated with him.

It was not many months before both Thomas and Alexander Campbell began to see that the Association of Washington, in spite of its intention not to be a church, was almost sure to become one and thereby contribute to the disunity that they were trying to overcome.

About a year after the Association was formed, Thomas Campbell applied to the Presbyterian Synod of Pittsburgh to be taken into its membership as an individual communicant and a minister. This was not the Seceder synod from which he had been dismissed but a synod of the main Presbyterian body. However, his application was rejected.

One may well wonder whether the movement known as the Disciples of Christ would have come into existence if Thomas Campbell had been readmitted into the Presbyterian Church. Once when I was making an historical address before one of our seminaries on an anniversary occasion, the late Dr. Henry Sloane Coffin, then President of Union Theological Seminary and formerly minister of the Madison Avenue Presbyterian Church in New York City, was sitting behind me. When I related that Thomas Campbell had been denied readmittance into the Presbyterian Church, Dr. Coffin arose and said that if the Disciples of Christ were to apply to the Presbyterian Church of the U.S.A. for admission now that he could almost assure us that we would be accepted.

Soon after this rejection Thomas and Alexander Campbell led the members of the Christian Association of Washington to constitute themselves into the Brush Run Church and establish themselves at Bethany, West Virginia. Alexander Campbell was ordained to the ministry of this church a few months after it was established.

It is to be emphasized that the Campbells had too profound a conception of the church to designate their society as a church when they were first ejected from the Seceder branch of the Presbyterian Church. It was only after they were denied readmission into the main body of the Presbyterian Church that they felt impelled to constitute a church in which they could worship and preach, and receive the Lord's Supper and administer baptism.

At this time the question of baptism by immersion had not yet risen. However, it was this question that had to be faced in the logic of their declaration, "Where the Scripture speaks we speak, and where the Scripture is silent we are silent," that led the Campbells and their associates in the newly established Brush Run Church to seek fellowship with Baptist churches. Prior to the raising of this question, however, they had not satisfied themselves as to a larger church relationship. Their separateness could not be condoned in the light of their concern for the unity of the church of Jesus Christ.

But even the briefest resume of Disciple history has to make place for the story of how immersion came to be adopted by the new church, how it gave them a false sense of affinity with Baptist churches and how it led to their affiliation with the Baptist churches for a few years. They were a part of the Baptist fellowship long enough for many people now to assume that the Disciple movement came out of the Baptist Churches.

No one can say what the position of the Campbells and their associates would have been on the question of immersion if they had been permitted to remain in the Presbyterian Church. Their record up until the time of their separation from that church and their subsequent behavior shows clearly that they were never afraid to take a position for conscience's sake. There is a question, however, whether they would have pursued their study of infant baptism with the same concern if they had remained in the Presbyterian Church. Their underlying conviction was that there should be unity in the church of Jesus Christ, and they were reluctant to insist on measures that were divisive. But when their connection with the Presbyterian Church was broken and they had determined to found their new church on the teaching and practice of the New Testament they were impelled to restudy the question of baptism.

Some of the members of the Christian Association of
Washington openly questioned the validity of infant baptism
when the Association in 1810 made application for union
with the Presbyterians, but it seems that the Campbells were
not among them. These few members, however, did not press
the matter. When the Synod of Pittsburgh charged that
Thomas Campbell had said that infant baptism was unscriptural and a matter of indifference he answered that
"neither pedo-baptism nor anti-pedo-baptism availeth anything but a new creature."

However, at least three members of the Brush Run Church
declined communion at the first service of the new church
because they had not been baptized, that is, they had not been
sprinkled in infancy. Before they would commune they requested baptism by immersion. It seems then that it was
agreed that immersion would be the only baptism administered to adults by the Brush Run Church. At the time it
appears that the question of baptism of infants was not
pressed. In June 1811 Alexander Campbell said: "As I am
sure it is unscriptural to make this matter a term of communion, I let it slip. I wish to think and let think on these
matters." [1] It was when his first child was born on March
13, 1812 that he went into a thorough study of the matter and
concluded that the sprinkling of infants did not constitute
baptism because it was the application of an unauthorized
form to an incompetent subject. Garrison and DeGroot say:
"This answered negatively the question about baptising his
infant, and it also swept away the concept of re-baptism. To
immerse those who had been sprinkled was not re-baptism

[1] "Memoirs of Alexander Campbell" by Robert Richardson. Vol. I., p. 392,
J. B. Lippincott & Company, 1868.

but baptism. He concluded therefore that he himself was un-
baptized."

Three months later, on June 12, 1812, father and son,
Thomas and Alexander Campbell, their wives and three other
members of the Brush Run Church were immersed by a
Baptist preacher. It was in this natural and undogmatic way
that baptism by immersion, and the baptism of adults only,
came to be the practice, first of the Brush Run Church, and
then of the Disciples of Christ in their subsequent history.

It was the adoption of baptism by immersion that brought
the Brush Run Church into a favorable position with the
Baptists, and at the same time created a gulf between them
and other denominations. For seventeen years, beginning
with the admission of the Brush Run Church into the Red
Stone Baptist Association in the autumn of 1813, the Disciples
of Christ were identified with the Baptist denomination but
this relationship was always tenuous, uncertain and never
happy either for the Baptists or the Disciples.

Alexander Campbell came under strong suspicion of the
Baptists after he substituted for another speaker at a meeting
of the Red Stone Baptist Association in 1816 and preached
what became his famous "Sermon of the Law." In this sermon
Campbell struck at the prevailing belief that a person could
open the Bible at random with the assurance that wherever
he pointed his finger to a verse, God would speak to him
there through His Word. Campbell was a forerunner of the
scholarly and devout Biblical critics who have clarified the
Bible to later generations. He showed that the Old Testament
has to be read in the light of God's revelation in Christ, as
recorded in the Gospels and rest of the New Testament.

The position that Alexander Campbell took in this sermon
concerning Biblical interpretation seemed to some who heard

him a dangerous teaching, and suspicion of him was spread among Baptist Churches. Some things that he said, however, were congenial to the Baptists. His argument that any connection or alliance between Church and State, as in the old covenant of Jehovah with the Hebrews, is contrary to the character of Christianity, met with their hearty approval. The Baptists agreed with him further when he denied that there is an analogy between circumcision of the Old Testament and Baptism of the New Testament.

But in 1829 when the Baptists withdrew fellowship from the Disciples they drew up eight accounts against the so-called "Reformers":

1. Reformers say there is no salvation without baptism.
2. They administer baptism to any who will say that Jesus Christ is the Son of God.
3. They do not wait for direct operation of the Holy Spirit on the mind prior to baptism.
4. They claim that baptism procures remission of sins, a gift of the Holy Spirit.
5. They say that Scriptures are the only evidence for interpreting Christ.
6. They say that obedience places it in God's power to elect anyone to salvation.
7. They say that no creed is necessary for the Church but the Scriptures as they stand.
8. They say that all baptized persons have the right to administer the ordinance of baptism.

We review now, very briefly, the history of the movement led by Barton W. Stone which joined with the Campbell movement in 1832.

Stone, like the Campbells, was a Presbyterian but it seems

that from the time of his ordination, and even before, he had trouble with two doctrines of his church: total depravity and divine election. It was in the extreme and radical interpretation of these doctrines that he found his difficulty. It is not likely that Stone would have been disaffected from the Presbyterian teaching on these matters as they are interpreted by that denomination today.

This is a place to state, what we shall amplify later, that in the doctrine of divine election, which in its severe interpretation became a paralyzing fatalism, we have the background from which the Disciples of Christ moved with vigor and evangelistic zeal to give hope to people that they themselves could do something about their salvation.

Barton Stone joined four other Presbyterian preachers to organize the independent Springfield Presbytery in 1803. Their Springfield is now Springdale, ten miles north of Cincinnati, Ohio. They issued a hundred page pamphlet with the uninviting title, "An Abstract of an Apology for Renouncing the Jurisdiction of the Synod of Kentucky, Being a Compendious View of Faith."

Three important points were made in this voluminous and heavy document:

1. Christ died for all as against a limited atonement for the elect.
2. The Gospel itself is the means of regeneration and faith and is the act by which any man, if he will, can lay hold of that means.
3. Faith is the natural man's belief in testimony—a rational, as against a mystical, conception of faith.

Less than a year after these five leaders had formed their presbytery, they brought it to an end and issued a document called "The Last Will and Testament of the Springfield Presbytery." But the arguments in this remarkable instrument showed that this was not the end but really the beginning of their main effort.

It was at the meeting of June 28, 1804, when "The Last Will and Testament" was formulated that the name "Christian" was adopted. The intention in taking this name was to avoid all sectarian designations.

Eight items were "willed" in "The Last Will and Testament":

1. That this body die, be dissolved and sink into union with the Body of Christ at large;
2. That every congregation be independent in the choice and support of its minister and the discipline of its members;
3. That the Bible alone should be the guide and standard of the church;
4. That ministers are not to be called "Reverend";
5. That ministers are to obtain license from God to preach the simple Gospel;
6. That ministers are to be supported by free-will offerings;
7. That ministers are not to have a written call or subscription;
8. That the Synod of Kentucky is exhorted to examine every suspect and suspend every heretic "that the oppressed may go free and taste the sweets of Gospel liberty."

At the end of 1804 there were at least thirteen Christian Churches in north central Kentucky and about seven in southwestern Ohio that had affiliated with the new movement.

It was not until 1824 that Alexander Campbell on a visit to Kentucky met for the first time Barton Stone. After the Baptist churches withdrew fellowship from the Disciples (before this happened, Disciples had taken over hundreds of Baptist churches), the Christian Church under Stone leadership and the Disciple Churches under Campbell drew closer together. They were formally merged into one body in Lexington, Kentucky in 1832.

The writer believes that it would be well at this point to include a more objective appraisal of the early history of this movement than would be expected from a Disciple. We quote therefore, from Dr. Roland Bainton's book, *The Social Sources of Denominationalism.* In a chapter on "Sectionalism and Denominationalism," Dr. Bainton shows how the Baptists and Methodists influenced the religious life of this nation in its earlier years. Then he goes on to say:

"The third great church of the West which took the leadership of the religious life of the nation away from the eastern denominations during the frontier period was the native born church of the Disciples of Christ. Methodists and Baptists accommodated themselves to conditions of the frontier and profited greatly by the harmony of their temper with its spirit; but the Disciples of Christ were a true product of the West. They were the joint result of various frontier movements, beginning with the republican Methodist revolt of James O'Kelly, the dissolution of the schismatic Springfield Presbytery, and the subsequent attempt of Marshall and Stone to organize the frontier Christians into an undenominational church, and ending with the attempt of the erstwhile Presbyterian, then Baptist, preacher, Alexander Campbell to unite

all Disciples of Christ on the basis of a frontier faith. Like
the Baptists and Methodists the Disciples used the methods
of the revival, fostered immediacy in religious experience
through appeal to the emotions, adopted lay preaching, ordained their clergymen without requiring theological education, and organized their churches on the sectarian principle.

"In all of these respects they represented the frontier spirit.
In their effort to overcome the divisions of denominationalism by rejecting creeds and seeking to found a united church
on the sole standard of the Bible, they represented a frontier
tendency which did not come to expression in the two rival
churches. The frontier not only divided its pioneers from
the established churches of the East but also impressed upon
them a common pattern of religious life and a common religious symbolism.

"The camp meeting was an early form of denominational
cooperation in which Presbyterian, Methodist and Baptist
preachers united. The conversions which took place, whether
in response to Calvinist preaching or to Arminian appeals,
were of the same type. The hymns which were sung, the
prayers which were offered, the symbols of heaven and hell
which were employed, the sins which were condemned, and
the righteousness which was portrayed, were the hymns,
prayers, symbols, sins, and virtues of the frontier—not those
of any special group.

"Furthermore, as in the case in almost every migration,
adherence of various sects previously isolated, was thrown
together on the frontier and achieved a social unity which
was bound to affect their religious prejudices and division.
Despite the similarity of their piety, Methodists and Baptists could not overcome the inherited difference between
their churches, supported as these were by the rivalries of

preachers. It remained for an American-born church to express the common character of frontier faith. It was not the common character of the Christian or even of an American version of that religion, that was expressed in it. Practices of the churches of established communities, their liturgies, their institutional character, their philosophical defense of the faith, their federal or Episcopal organizations, were scarcely regarded as Christian by the early Disciples; only that interpretation of the New Testament which appeared reasonable from the point-of-view of the West was regarded as truly Christian. In this instance, as in many other movements of a similar sort, the fact that the New Testament is the book of a first generation of disciples and therefore one in which neither the institutional character of a religious community nor the claims of family solidarity could come to very explicit expression, was naturally overlooked—much to the advantage of the desired interpretation.

"The church of the Disciples remained a western, but primarily a middle western church. It was not a frontier faith in quite the same way as were Methodism and Baptist movements. Not only did it start its course later than those, achieving organization only after the frontier had passed hundreds of miles further inland, but it lacked much of the emotional fervor that these other denominations possessed. It was somewhat more interested in the social principle of union than in the individual principle of the salvation of souls. Perhaps this was the reason why it was less aggressive than its rivals. It was representative of a West that had passed the storm and stress period of social adolescence and was recovering from its useful extremities of hope and fear without having lost the characteristic features that the formative years had impressed upon it."

FOUR

BELIEVER'S BAPTISM

SINCE THE Disciples of Christ are one of the relatively few communions that practices baptism by immersion and because their doctrine of baptism seems not to be well known even by leaders and scholars in other denominations we undertake here to state and substantiate the Disciple teaching on this question.

I cannot claim to represent the whole, or even the majority, Disciple constituency as I deal with this subject. I have been criticized often and have been under attack a few times by some of my brethren because of what they consider my too liberal view of this matter.

For many years I have been on record as being an "open membership" minister. I led the Union Avenue Christian Church in St. Louis, Missouri, of which I was minister for more than sixteen years, to practice open membership. The church of which I am now pastor in New York City has been an open membership church for many years.

By open membership the Disciples mean the practice of

receiving unimmersed Christians from other denominations into full membership of a Disciples of Christ Church. We do not have a record of open membership churches but we are sure that their number is increasing. Those that are avowedly open membership could be counted but there are many others that quietly accommodate themselves to the growing practice of receiving members who have not been immersed. It is not fair to accuse these churches and their ministers of insincerity or subterfuge. If a vote on whether or not to receive the unimmersed into membership were forced in some of these churches the issue would be sharply drawn with unhappy results. Where the issue is not forced, many of these churches will accept into their membership the occasional unimmersed Christian who for some specific reason, such as uniting his family in one church, wishes to be a member but is not ready to be rebaptized by immersion.

For so long the Disciples have made immersion a basis of membership that many present-day Disciples, who have never thought through their position, echo the feelings of their parents and grandparents and make it difficult for their churches to practice open membership.

While I have been on the liberal side of the question of inclusive membership (I prefer to call it that rather than open membership), I must confess to my friends in the ecumenical fellowship that I would find it impossible to accept the pastorate of a church if to do so I were charged with the responsibility of baptizing infants. This may sound like a repudiation of the principles of the ecumenical movement and of my activities in behalf of Christian unity. However, as we say elsewhere in this book, it is not the spirit of the ecumenical movement to insist that churches give up any of their basic convictions in order to belong to the larger

fellowship. Rather, it is the spirit of the ecumenical movement to ask for the witness of the participating churches on
the matters that have deep meaning to them.

The practice of the churches that I have served on the
question of receiving members into the church, I believe, is
clearly defined and defensible. We affirm that we shall not
make baptism by immersion a basis of fellowship. We declare
that a person who is satisfied with his own baptism and
shows by the fruits of his faith and life that he is a Christian,
will be welcomed into the membership of our church. However, the church itself does not baptize infants because it
considers that baptism should be received voluntarily when
one is old enough to profess his own faith in Christ and seek
membership in the church. This we refer to as "believer's
baptism."

We practice believer's baptism by immersion because this
was the baptism with which our Lord was baptized, and
further, because immersion symbolizes in dramatic and
memorable form that which takes place in the heart of a
person who in faith gives himself to the Lordship of Jesus
Christ. While I was only a boy I made my confession of
faith in Christ before the church and then received baptism.
My baptismal experience is marked in my life with inerasable
memory and with an emotion that has remained with me.

The Disciples have been accused, especially by some other
immersionist groups, as believing in "water salvation." While
there may have been in our history some poorly educated, un-
informed and fanatical ministers who believed and taught
that baptism is, in its own physical aspects, effective for salvation, I assure our readers that no Disciple minister of
my acquaintance holds that the water has anything to do
with the salvation of the person receiving baptism. However,

we believe that one who has become convinced that God was in Christ and in faith accepts Christ as his Lord and Savior confirms in his baptism this transforming and lasting experience.

Disciples have not had a profound conception of the sacramental nature of baptism even as they have not been greatly concerned with the sacramental character of the communion of the Lord's Supper. They do not think of either of these so much as a means of grace as a visible representation of the invisible covenant between God and the person who has given himself in faith to Jesus Christ.

Baptism has no meaning apart from the reality of a new experience of God that results from a new-found faith in Jesus Christ. But when one has found that faith in Christ and through that faith has received grace to know himself as a true child of God, baptism becomes an act of great significance.

First of all it is an act which Jesus required of Himself at the hands of John the Baptist. John had taken over this old symbol of cleaning, immersion, and made it a baptism of repentance. Surely any one of us would have taken the same stand that John took first, when he refused to baptize Jesus, saying that he, John, had need to be baptized of Jesus.

Why did Jesus insist on this baptism? Why would He, who had not sinned, identify Himself with sinful people? It was for this reason that God sent Him into the world. It is my conviction that Jesus insisted on John's baptism of repentance because He was taking upon Himself guilt for the sins of the world. By this baptism He identified Himself with the guilty.

We cannot say that baptism washed away the guilt because Jesus continued to bear the guilt for sinful men until He had done the last thing that He could do to redeem sinful men, which was the bearing of the Cross. Nevertheless, the baptism of Jesus at the hands of John the Baptist was a sign that He had recognized His guilt and must identify Himself with guilty men. John the Baptist had the insight to see only that Jesus had not need of repentance; he lacked this deeper insight that Jesus in order to lead men to repentance must identify Himself with their guilt.

Any person who is of an age to know even in an elementary way what it means to confess his faith in Jesus Christ as his Lord and Savior and then asks the church for baptism, would be called on to consider why Jesus required baptism of John the Baptist.

It is important, I believe, to lead candidates for Baptism to see that they are to receive baptism not only at the command of Jesus Christ but also because of His example. It is hard to see how baptism, other than believer's baptism by immersion, can give one the feeling of sharing in the baptism of Jesus.

Baptism by immersion, when fully interpreted, is a declaration of the death and resurrection of our Lord. The Apostle Paul saw in Baptism the symbol of this central truth of the Gospel. Every one who has made a true confession of his faith in Jesus Christ and receives baptism by immersion at the hands of the church declares again by this vivid symbol, this greatest truth of the Gospel.

For this reason, unless there are extenuating circumstances, baptism should not be administered privately. Baptism was given to the church. It is administered by the church. It is a proclamation of the truth entrusted to the church. Therefore, baptism should be administered where and when it can be observed, where it can bear its dramatic witness to the most important event in human history.

There is a third symbolic meaning to baptism by immersion. It is not only the symbol of sharing with Jesus Who shares guilt with us, and the symbol of "Good News" that the church has to declare; it is also the symbol of the redemption which the Christian experiences through his faith in Christ. All that is not of Christ is buried. The Christian has arisen to a new creation. Old things have passed away. All things have become new. This burying of the old and rising to the new is due to being baptized into Christ: "Do you not know that all of us who have been baptized into Christ Jesus were baptized into his death? We were buried therefore with him by baptism into death, so that as Christ was raised from the dead by the glory of the Father, we too might walk in newness of life." Romans 6:3, 4.

Disciples of Christ do not want to make baptism by immersion the basis of fellowship with other Christians. I hardly know any person who is in the true Disciple tradition who would disassociate himself from other Christians. I know of no Disciple who would not readily acknowledge that in all other churches there are true disciples of the Lord, Jesus Christ.

However, Disciples do not believe that their exalting of the ordinance of baptism by immersion is an inconsequential thing. For the reasons given, immersion has great meaning to the Disciples of Christ, and they have a sincere desire to witness to the significance of baptism as they see it.

In this ecumenical time Disciples are finding the meaning of the traditions and practices of other denominations. For instance, the great historic liturgies which earlier Disciples neglected or rejected altogether are now being studied, and many of their elements are appropriated in the worship of the churches of the Disciples of Christ.

While the Disciples do not accept the doctrine of the ministry of the Anglican Church, their own conception of the ministry has been profoundly affected by the study of the meaning of ordination in that church. The conception of the church itself, the Biblical doctrine of the church, has been influenced by our association in the ecumenical movement with churches of older traditions than those of the Disciples. Again let us say that it is the spirit of the ecumenical movement to seek out the reasons why other churches love what they love and emphasize what they emphasize.

But even as the Disciples are ready to learn from other denominations, they believe that they have an important witness for the other churches in the ecumenical movement. One of the Disciple practices to which Disciples call the attention of these other churches is believer's baptism by immersion, with its beauty and symbolic meaning.

I believe that since Disciples have become less dogmatic in their preaching of immersion and shown an increased willingness to receive the unimmersed from other churches into their fellowship, other denominations are becoming more interested in the Disciples' witness of their practice.

There are evidences that a restudy of baptism with particular attention to the question of believer's baptism (this, more than the physical form of baptism) may be getting under way in the theological world. Both Barth and Brunner have raised the question in some of their more recent writings.

I do not wish to conclude this part of our discussion without acknowledging the very deep emotion that stirs in the hearts of parents when they bring their infant to the baptismal font. If the parents, instructed by their church, believe that original sin is cancelled by this baptism, I can understand why they would not consent to the postponement of the sacrament until the child was old enough to confess his own Christian faith and consent to baptism.

However, I do not believe that there are many people these days who believe that the God and Father of the Lord Jesus Christ would lay upon the life of an innocent babe the guilt of some original sin. This is so tremendous in its implication that if it were true I cannot conceive how this same God would call the record clear because the parents had submitted the baby to this simple liturgical act.

It is my observation that the baptism of infants has in the mind of most of the churches that practice it, a very beautiful meaning. It is the dedication by Christian parents of their child to God, with prayer that they themselves may be worthy of the great gift of parenthood; and, by their teaching and example, guide their child into the church and to the development of a full Christian life.

If this is the case I hope that the ecumenical church may bring its constituent denominations to consider, unhurriedly and without prejudice, making of this initial ceremony a simple dedication service, delaying baptism until the child himself, is old enough to experience its meaning.

FIVE

THE COMMUNION OF THE LORD'S SUPPER

THE Disciples of Christ emphasize the words, "This do in remembrance of me," in the observance of the Lord's Supper. To us it is a simple fellowship meal. The Loaf and the Cup are the reminders of the suffering of the Lord, Jesus Christ. This suffering He had to endure in order to fulfill the mission for which God sent Him to the earth.

It is almost impossible for a Disciple to comprehend how the simple meal in the Upper Room in Jerusalem has been transformed and mutilated into the elaborate mystery of the Mass of the Roman Catholic Church.

To us what happened in the Upper Room was so natural. Jesus took the unleavened bread of the Jewish Passover and said to His disciples something like this: "From this time on, this bread will have a new signfiance to you. It will be my body which is broken for you." And then He took the cup of light wine and poured it out, at the same time speaking in this manner: "This too will have a significance different from that which it holds in the Passover of our people.

54

From now on, it will be my blood which was shed for you."

These elements, the Bread and the Wine, are reminders of Him who was persecuted for righteousness' sake, and in the bearing of His persecution revealed the character of God, Whose Son He was and Whose Spirit He had allowed to fully possess Him.

The centering of the mind on Christ, with the aid of these visible symbols, makes the communicant receptive to the grace of God—grace which God is always ready to give to those who will accept it.

It is the conviction of the Disciples of Christ that the Lord's Supper belongs in every Sunday morning service of worship. The church of which I am the minister in New York City, has observed the Communion every Sunday from the beginning of its history, now 147 years.

Many rural churches that have the services of a minister only once or twice a month meet regularly every Sunday for the celebration of the Lord's Supper.

In all candor it must be acknowledged that this frequent observance of the Communion in Disciples' churches has taken from our members the sense of expectancy with which members of other churches await their Communion Sunday. Furthermore, we must confess that our people have not been disciplined as they should in the preparation of themselves for the Communion service.

It is disappointing to the minister of a Disciples church to know that many people who are about to receive the sacred emblems from the Lord's Table have given no thought to this Communion until the very moment when the prayers are offered at the Table, and I am afraid that some of them even receive the emblems and eat and drink them while their minds are on other things.

But while this is true about some of our members, many others—very many—anticipate prayerfully every Sunday's Communion service; and on those Sundays when they are deprived of the Communion because they are ill or visit a church where the Lord's Supper is not spread on that particular Sunday, they feel the lack of it all week long.

In Disciple churches the Communion can be administered to the congregation by lay elders or other lay members. The fact that this can be done bears upon the Disciple conception of the ministry which will be discussed in another chapter. In the church that I now serve, the minister himself, never presides at the Communion Table nor offers the Communion prayer. The service of Communion comes in this particular church at the very close of the service as the climactic event of corporate worship. The minister goes to his seat before the Communion service begins. Two lay elders make their way to the Table to preside over the Communion.

One of the elders speaks briefly of the significance of this Memorial Meal, the Lord's Supper. There is no specified ritual for the service, but in the majority of instances the meaning of the service and the invitation to partake of the Supper are spoken in the language of the New Testament. The other elder offers the prayer both for the Loaf and the Cup. The prayer is one of his own choosing; most often, I am inclined to believe, he himself has formulated it.

In some of our churches, I regret to say, the elders themselves are not prepared as they should be when they come to preside over the Communion. Either they repeat the same prayer, which has been of their own making, Sunday after Sunday, or they take a cue from the sermon for an impromptu prayer.

But more and more in Disciple churches, due to the education of the elders by the ministers and because of a new sense of the meaning of liturgy, elders are taught to draw from the great treasury of prayers that are available in the universal church of our Lord.

The very simplicity of the Communion service in a Disciples of Christ church, emphasized sometimes by the faltering leadership of sincere laymen, is impressive to the congregation by the fact that plain people with all their frailties and limitations have access to this sacred Table. Here if their hearts are pure and their desire to commune with their Lord is strong, they can renew their strength, mount up with wings as eagles, run and not be weary, walk and not faint.

In their inclusive invitation to all Christians to share with them in the Lord's Supper, the Disciples of Christ have not been consistent with their historic exclusion from membership in their churches of those who have not been immersed. Those of us who have taken the more liberal position about baptism have justified our position in part by reference to the historic practice of an inclusive fellowship at the Communion Table.

It is readily seen that the Disciple position on the Communion puts up no blocks to fellowship with any other denomination. The question of the efficacy of the ordination or the lack of ordination on the part of those who preside over the Communion does not deter a Disciple from communion with his brethren of other churches. Not even the interpretation of the meaning of the Communion by another church, when it differs from the prevailing Disciple conception, prevents a Disciple from taking part in the service.

In fact, Disciples do not insist on a particular interpretation for their own members, although as we have said, most of them think of it as a simple Memorial. We believe that

it is far better for Christians through habitual observance
of the Lord's Supper to fathom deeper and deeper its mean-
ings. The Holy Spirit itself operates in and through the
Communion service; and there is the promise of Christ Himself, that when the Spirit is come, He will lead us into truth.
We believe that every Christian, however deficient his understanding, should be welcomed to the Communion Table
where he can find for himself what God has provided. After
all, it is not what any one, or any one church, says that the
Communion means that is of supreme significance; rather it
is what God has given in the Communion which earnest
seekers will find if they are faithful in their attendance at
the Sacred Meal.

In Disciple churches the Bread and Wine of the Communion are served to the congregation by the deacons who
first receive these emblems from the elders. I have no way
of knowing how many churches place the Communion at the
close of the service as the church which I serve does. Every
congregation determines for itself where in the service the
Communion will be observed. Many churches celebrate the
Communion before the sermon. There are reasons that can
be given to justify placing the Communion at either place.
If it comes in the early part of the service of worship you can
reason that it is good to have it there so that the people will
be better prepared to hear the Word of God in the sermon.
If the Communion is placed at the end of the service you can
reason that the preceding worship rightly should lead to this
climactic experience.

At the International Convention of Christian Churches
(Disciples of Christ) the Communion of the Lord's Supper
is always celebrated on a Sunday afternoon. Sometimes conventions begin on Friday night or Saturday, and then it is

anticipated that the Sunday Communion will provide inspiration for all the remainder of the sessions. Sometimes the convention closes on Sunday and then the Communion is thought of as the climactic service toward which the whole convention moves.

This Communion Service is always held in the largest auditorium in the city. It is so carefully planned and rehearsed that the details of the serving of the thousands of people who assemble for it are hardly observed by the communicants. I have seen eight or ten thousand people served and the whole liturgy of the Communion Service completed within a little more than a half hour.

There is always the danger of the large Communion Service at the convention being looked upon as a spectacle. I am sure that many people outside the Disciple fellowship who read about it in the newspapers get that impression. But those who share prayerfully in the service, knowing that the important thing is the individual's own communion with his Lord, nevertheless, experience an increased operation of the Spirit that seems to be in proportion to the great number of communicants.

In Chicago a few years ago when the Disciples of Christ and the American Baptist Churches were holding simultaneous conventions with several joint sessions, these two great denominations celebrated together the Lord's Supper with a huge congregation that filled the Stockyards Auditorium. Because the Communion as practiced by the Baptists has to be held under the auspices of a local church the program indicated that one of the Chicago Baptist churches along with the Disciples of Christ, was providing this Communion Service. Baptists are known not to be as ready for union Communion Services as Disciples and there was on the part of many Baptists a genuine concern about this service, but the Spirit of the Living Christ was so evident there that both Baptists and Disciples felt that they had been singularly blessed.

The Disciples of Christ have been distressed that at the great ecumenical conferences it has not yet been possible to have a Communion Service for the whole assembly. There are obstacles relating to ordination and the nature of the Communion itself that stand in the way. However, at the Second Assembly of the World Council of Churches at Evanston in 1954 it was found that three or four Communion Services, according to as many traditions, were able to minister to nearly all the delegates. It is difficult for Disciples of Christ to comprehend why it is not possible to break down the ecclesiastical and theological barriers in the spirit of the Simple Meal in the Upper Room in Jerusalem so that all Christians can join in the Communion. How has the simplicity of the early fellowship developed into the hard forms and fixed practices that divide the church?

A number of years ago while I was preparing a class of children for church membership I put the meaning of the Communion in the simplest possible terms and as I did so I was struck by the thought that I should put this meaning no less simply to myself and other adults in the church. Among other things I said to the children that before every Communion Service they should think back to the time of their latest Communion and be ready to confess, first to themselves and then to God, the things they had done which they ought not to have done and the things which they had left undone which they ought to have done. Furthermore I suggested to the children that they put into their minds a picture of themselves as they would be if they were to allow Christ to guide them at all times. And then I proposed to them that while they were in the Communion Service they would make this confession to God and hold this picture in their minds.

The most solemn counsel that any minister can give to his congregation for the Communion is that which the Apostle Paul gave to the Corinthian Church when he said, "He that eateth and drinketh without discerning the body of Christ, eateth and drinketh condemnation to himself." This means, I believe, that if you allow your mind to wander rather than centering it on Christ your Communion is only a pretense, and, like any other lie, damaging. It is a startling thought that the Communion might be hurtful rather than helpful.

But while communicants need to be warned of the danger of a careless participation in the Communion they must be assured also that they are invited to the Lord's Table not because they are strong but because they are weak, not because they are righteous but because they are sinful and need the mercy of God's forgiveness.

This, I believe, is the way that most ministers and lay members among the Disciples of Christ look upon the Communion. To them the simple Memorial Meal that was instituted in the Upper Room in Jerusalem should be preserved in its simplicity.

SIX

THE NATURE OF THE CHURCH
AND ITS MINISTRY

THE Disciples of Christ determined in the beginning of their movement to by-pass the historic creeds of the church, and in fact the whole history of the church and go back to its Apostolic origin. However, they were saved from many of the errors of that independence by their earnest desire to have fellowship with all Christian people. The two missions of the Disciples that were set forth in the beginning of their history to restore New Testament Christianity and to witness to the unity of the church, have tended to balance one another. Their relative independence of Protestant denominationalism in the early years gave to the movement a vitality that was unhampered by historical considerations but their passion for unity has increasingly subjected them to the witness of other denominations.

It obviously was a mistake for the Disciples to think that they could cancel out the history of the church in the centuries intervening between the Apostolic church and the beginnings of their movement. And yet this very freedom from tradition made them susceptible to and eager for the leading of the Holy Spirit beyond those who are bound by the crystallizations of their creed.

This benefit has been more in evidence in recent decades. At first the Disciples were bound by their own literal interpretation of the New Testament. Only as they have been freed from this by accepting the results of Biblical scholarship have they come into the fullness of their freedom to seek and follow fresh insights, guided as we believe by the Holy Spirit.

At this point, however, we must distinguish between the trends of liberal and conservative groups within the Disciple movement. The Disciples have their own traditionalists who have encumbered their group with unwritten creeds that formalize and dogmatize the early beliefs and practices of the movement. This conservative segment has isolated itself more and more from the main body of Disciples.

The trend of the main body has been in pursuit of the unity of the church and, therefore, has associated itself at every opportunity with interdenominational action and with the ecumenical movement. This association has made this main body of the Disciples appreciative of the history, the traditions, the doctrines and even the organization of other denominations.

It appears to me that the clearest approach to the Disciples' conception of the church is by way of historical references to their ministry. Although, as we have tried to show, Thomas Campbell proved by his reluctance to call his "Christian Association of Washington" a church, that he and his followers had a profound conception of the church. Nevertheless, the church was pushed into the background of their thinking by their concern for the message of the preacher.

Nearly all of the earliest preachers were traveling evangelists who gave their attention to the winning of converts rather than the development of churches. Of course, churches came into being and grew strong because of these converts; but still the preachers were more concerned in proclaiming the way of salvation to individuals than in nurturing the churches.

In the beginning the Disciples were not insistent upon the ordination of their ministers. However, it should be noted that leaders of the movement, both from the Campbell branch and the Stone branch, were men who had been well trained according to the standards of their day.

Thomas Campbell, after deciding to become a minister, took the three-year classical course that was then offered at the University of Glasgow. After that he took the regular seminary course offered by his branch of the Presbyterian Church which, according to Garrison and DeGroot, consisted of five terms of eight weeks each, all of the instruction being given by one professor who was also pastor of a local church.

Alexander Campbell received his early education from his father who was principal of and teacher in his own seminary in Ireland. Alexander Campbell also had one year at the University of Glasgow. There he came under the guidance of the Reverend Greville Ewing who was in charge of a training school in Glasgow for lay preachers.

A few years ago I was invited to preach two sermons in the Lady Glenarchy's Church in the neighborhood of the University of Edinburgh. In 1802 Greville Ewing was asked to resign from the pulpit of Lady Glenarchy's Church because of certain opinions which he held that were contrary to the general views of his congregation. Both the congregation and the visiting minister took account of the fact that there was that day in the pulpit of Lady Glenarchy's Church a minister from the United States who in a sense was a spiritual descendant of a preacher whom their church had dismissed from its pulpit.

They were not at all clear as to why a minister of so fine a personal character and outstanding scholarly attainments should have been dismissed more than one hundred and thirty years before. The reasons come to light in a book by J. A. Haldane, published in 1805, a book with this long title: *A View of the Social Worship and Ordinances Observed by the First Christians, Drawn from the Scriptures Alone; Being an Attempt to Enforce their Divine Obligation; and to Represent the Guilty and Evil Consequences of Neglecting Them.*

When Alexander Campbell entered the University of Glasgow late in 1808 he found that Ewing had introduced this book into his seminary course. According to Garrison and DeGroot, this book and that of Glass and Sandeman which Ewing taught, gave a "general impetus to religious reformation of a radical sort and on a strictly Biblical basis."

In these books also were such specific ideas as the independence of each local congregation and the rejection of all clerical privileges and dignities without rejecting the ministry itself; the right and duty of laymen to have a part in edifying as well as ruling the church; a plurality of elders; a conception of faith as the belief of testimony, an act of which any man is capable by applying his natural intelligence to the evidence supplied by Scripture; and the weekly observance of the Lord's Supper. All of these ideas found their way into the Disciples' movement.

Alexander Campbell preached before he was ordained. Neither he nor his father saw anything wrong in this. Alexander, while not minimizing the significance of ordination, saw no reason why a layman should not preach. When the Christian Association of Washington formed itself into the Brush Run Church on May 14, 1811, Alexander Campbell was licensed to preach. On the next New Year's Day he was ordained to the ministry.

Garrison and DeGroot say: "It was implicit in the position of these reformers [the Campbells and their associates] that the distinction between clergy and laity was artificial, that it had no Scriptural warrant, and that it tended toward the domination of the church by a clerical cast. But there was recognition of the propriety of setting apart, by the imposition of hands, men who were to bear office in the church as elders or to devote their lives to the work of the ministry. For all his insistence upon the right of laymen to tell the good news of the Gospel, and all his resistance to anything like a clerical monopoly, Alexander Campbell saw the need of a responsible ministry, definitely commissioned by the church. Therefore he accepted a license to preach from the Brush Run Church on the very first day of its existence, and ordination seven months later."

Because there was no overall authority for Disciple churches it was easy for poorly equipped and unworthy men to impose themselves on local congregations. In many instances our churches suffered from the incompetence and vagaries of these men.

However from the time of the Campbells throughout our history, even when little or no emphasis was given to ordination, there has always been the insistence that ministers must be of the highest character. Perhaps it was because there was not the safeguard of ordination on which other churches relied that there was the most careful scrutiny of the personal life of men who offered themselves for the ministry.

One is reminded that the preparation for the ministry in the early and middle years of the nineteenth century, especially in the frontier sections of this country, was acquired in very much the same way as medical and legal students were trained. Lawyers in those days would take a young man into their offices to "read law," and the older lawyers themselves would determine when the young man was ready to go before the court to practice law. In a similar way young men went into the offices of older doctors to "read medicine." Our own family physician when I was a boy had been trained this way, and yet he was recognized as one of the leading doctors in the city. To be sure he had not stopped "reading medicine" when he began his practice; he continued his medical education throughout his long life. So it was with many ministers, not only of the Disciples of Christ, in that time. But their lack of schooling did not prevent many of them from getting a thorough Biblical education through their own diligent efforts.

Today I believe that there is no denomination that is more concerned about theological education than the Disciples. Our seminaries are allied with the American Association of Theological Schools, and right now, with the intention of constantly improving themselves, are weighing the reports that are coming from the Study of Theological Education in the United States and Canada, a study undertaken by the afore-named Association.

There is a growing insistence on the part of our congregationally governed churches that anyone who offers himself as a candidate for the ministry be ready to pursue his studies through college and seminary to the degree of Bachelor of Divinity. Many of our ministers go on to higher graduate degrees in leading undenominational seminaries or universities.

The character of the ministry is safeguarded with the growing practice of requiring persons wishing to take theological training to secure the approval of the elders of their local church. While any local church has the right in our congregational system to ordain one of its own sons or the man whom it has called to its pastorate, a precedent is developing for that church to call upon neighboring churches, first, to approve of the ordination and, then, to participate in the ordination service. In a city like St. Louis, which I know best after a pastorate there of more than sixteen years, almost any of our churches before ordaining a minister would call upon the Disciples Union, representing all our churches, to approve of and participate in the ordination.

In some states, preeminently Ohio, there is a growing sentiment and practice for the churches to look to the state organization and the state secretary especially, for approval of the person who seeks ordination. In the chapter in which we deal with the organizational life of the Disciples of Christ, we shall deal more fully with the growing importance of the office of state secretary.

Within some state organizations where the state secretary himself is not asked to approve of a person for ordination, there is a committee of the state convention which is accorded the right—as far as a convention can influence congregationally governed Disciples churches—of passing on the credentials of a candidate for ordination.

In some instances ministers have been ordained at state conventions, and in several of our recent international conventions there have been ordination services. I for one, while not repudiating such ordination services, do not approve of them because it is my belief that the church itself should ordain the minister. I do not feel that a convention is the proper setting for an ordination service, especially when it is assembled in a large civic auditorium as most of our international conventions are because of the great numbers of people who attend.

The Disciples of Christ do not hold to the doctrine of the Apostolic Succession. We see no special merit in an ordination where the laying on of hands derives its authority from the hands of previous bishops, back through the long and devious path of history, to the Apostolic Church. This, to us, is an altogether too mechanical conception of the ministry. And because of our great concern to realize the unity of the church of Jesus Christ, the insistence on Apostolic Succession by some denominations has to be viewed by us as one of the greatest stumbling blocks in the way of that goal. It is this doctrine more than anything else that prevents the representatives of the churches at an ecumenical conference from coming together in one Communion Service.

But while the Disciples of Christ reject the historical doctrine of Apostolic Succession as being entirely too mechanical they are coming, I believe, to see that the Christian ministry follows in a real succession or continuity. That is the continuity of the church itself through the successive generations. It is within this succession that ministers of all denominations and confessions of the church the world over, have been endowed with faith and power for their ministry.

There is available a kind of "grass roots" statement of the Disciples' conception of the nature of the church. Prior to the World Convention of the Disciples of Christ in Toronto in the summer of 1955, study groups in the United States, Canada, England, Australia and New Zealand had concerned themselves with the doctrines of the Christian faith. Reports were made on these studies at Toronto and following the discussion there, these reports were revised and published. One of these studies had to do with the church.

From this study it is evident that Disciples generally believe that the church is the creation of God, and that it was brought into being by His redemptive act of sending Jesus Christ into the world. By His life and teaching, His suffering, His death and His resurrection, Jesus revealed to man the nature of God.

The Christian Church is something more than a continuation of the old Israel. The Church in its New Testament significance could not have come into being prior to the resurrection of Christ. The proclamation of the Good News—in the New Testament term, the "kerygma"—was the heralding of what God had done for man in Jesus Christ.

The sermons in the Acts of the Apostles, the study notes, follow the same general outline: prophecy has been fulfilled; Jesus of Nazareth, sent from God, performed His ministry; He was put to death for our sins; and was raised gloriously. God offers forgiveness of sins to all who repent and turn to Him.

The report of the study takes note of two factors in the beginning of the church, and insists that the second was necessary to the first. The first was the proclamation of the Good News, the Gospel; and the second was the human response to it. True to the historic Disciple position, the report declares: "We scarcely can over-emphasize the importance of the Apostolic 'kerygma' and the human response to it as determining the character of the church in New Testament times. From this constitutive principle flows the unity of the church. The response of men, let it be noted, was to the "kerygma." It was not to a creedal statement of faith or to the theory of the atonement, or to a code of ethics, or to a church polity, or to a theory concerning the sacraments, or to an order of clergy, or to a theological explanation of the Christhood of Jesus. These matters came later—some of them after the church came into existence—but the response, by which humanly speaking, the church began, was to the "kerygma."

The report proceeds to show that the influence of the "kerygma" extended very clearly to the sacraments or ordinances of the church. These are two in number, baptism and the Lord's Supper. In outward form each of these in its own way corresponded to the "kerygma." Baptism, universally performed by immersion in water of those who had faith corresponded in form to the cardinal facts of "kerygma," the burial (following the death) and the resurrection of Christ. The Lord's Supper whose material elements of bread and wine were provided by the broken loaf and the shared cup, by its form drew attention to the saving grace of God offered to man in the self-giving death of Christ. The fact that all shared in these, displayed visibly the basic truth that the life of the church rested upon both God's offer and man's acceptance. Just as the "kerygma" must find response in faith, so the sacraments regulated in form by their correspondence to "kerygma" were to be received by those who had faith. In the New Testament there is no instance where either sacrament was administered to those with faith.

At this point, the report of the study, which is as near a consensus of Disciple beliefs as we have, deals with the nature of the ministry as it is derived from this conception of the church. The church could and did set apart for its ministry certain persons, such as Barnabas and Saul at Antioch, as

reported in Acts 13:1. Those who were chosen led the congregation in ways that are no longer clear in detail, but what
is clear is that the church, as the body of Christ, was itself a
ministry.

The men and women within its limits were individually
priests of God. It is stated in I Peter 2:5: "Like living stones
be yourselves built into a spiritual house, to be a holy priesthood." There is no evidence of the existence of a clerical
caste that he had the exclusive rights to interpret and trans-
mit the Word or to administer the sacraments. Evidence
is also lacking to indicate that the worship of the New Testament church included sacrifice in the sense of any form or
ceremony.

So important was the possession of the Holy Spirit, that
Paul (Acts 19:1-17) required repetition of baptism of those
who had been immersed but who had shown no knowledge
of the Holy Spirit. Those who had not the Spirit, according
to Paul, did not belong to Christ.

In whatever way the presence of the Spirit was manifest,
the presence and the power were the proof that God's redemptive work had been effective.

Apart from the church there could be no preaching, hence
no hearing and no faith; and if not faith then no real baptism
and no gift of the Holy Spirit. The New Testament assumes
that there is no salvation outside the church.

Still following this study, believing that it states what
Disciples generally believe, there is the assertion that the
church is not a local institution. A member of the Church
of Christ in Bilaspur, India, or the Methodist Church in
Leeds, England, or of any other individual church in any
country is not first of all an Indian or an Englishman, a
Disciple or a Methodist. Recent experience in ecumenical

conferences, added to that of many Christians under other conditions, demonstrates that there is a fellowship of Spirit that transcends the barriers of creed and custom.

These facts and the reality of fellowship make it evident that Christians have not been made Christians by their response to the distinctive beliefs and practices that separate them into the denominational churches. Rather they have been made children of God by their response in faith to the proclamation of the Gospel of Grace, that which is common to all churches.

Wherever the Word has been preached, wherever persons have responded to the proclamation of faith, wherever their lives display the fruits of the Spirit and they have been drawn into the true fellowship because of their common commitment to the one Lord, there the church exists.

The Disciples of Christ find in this, evidence of the truth of Thomas Campbell's own definition of the church of Christ as "consisting of all those in every place who make their profession of faith in Christ according to the Scriptures and who manifest the same by their tempers and conduct." If we define the church in its irreducible minimum in these terms, the church is as necessary to salvation today as it was in its beginning in the New Testament.

SEVEN

ORGANIZATION

BY ITS VERY nature, a congregationally governed church, like the Disciples of Christ, does not have and cannot have a strong central organization. Sometimes it is said that every Disciple church is a law unto itself, but this could not be absolutely true while these churches voluntarily associate themselves in a "brotherhood" or denomination.

Even those churches that have resisted all authority beyond the congregation and withdrawn from the fellowship of the main body of Disciples because of this issue have banded themselves together to strengthen one another in their resistance. Although they have withdrawn from the International Convention of Christian Churches (Disciples of Christ) they have felt the necessity of having an assembly of their own. Although they stopped reporting to the Year Book of the Disciples of Christ, they have begun to publish a Year Book of their own. They are finding it impossible not to give some loyalty to an organization beyond that of the local congregation.

The pattern of organization of the Disciples of Christ has evolved slowly, and is continually in the process of change. Perhaps it will never become fixed because of the nature of the church itself. Some of the more important national agencies of the Disciples of Christ have come into existence in comparatively recent times. This is true of the International Convention of Christian Churches (Disciples of Christ), which in its present form and function came into being in 1917 to serve the Disciple churches in the United States and Canada. This convention marks the present state of evolution of the first general convention of Disciples which was organized in 1849.

The preamble to the constitution of the present International Convention reads:

"Whereas, there is a widespread feeling among Disciples of Christ that a closer cooperation among their various missionary, educational, benevolent and other agencies and a more general fellowship in their common efforts for the extension of the Kingdom of God in the world, would result in greater efficiency:

"Therefore, we, members of churches of Disciples of Christ in convention assembled, reaffirming our steadfast adherence to the independence and autonomy of the local churches and disavowing any control over our congregations or missionary or educational or benevolent agencies other than that which is advisory, and inviting the fellowship of all brethren in the accomplishment of these ends, do hereby adopt the following: . . ."

The headquarters of the International Convention is in Indianapolis, Indiana. The function of the headquarters office is to coordinate the commissions and committees each year at the Convention Assembly, to compile the Year Book of the Disciples of Christ, and also to organize and present the annual International Convention Assembly.

Furthermore, the Convention office, through its Department of Public Relations, attempts to provide a united front for the Disciples of Christ to the secular news services.

The International Convention is directed by a board of directors of fifteen persons, five of whom are elected every year to serve a three-year term. The Convention elects its president to serve for a one-year term. The staff members include an executive secretary and assistant secretary, director of public relations and several office secretaries. Sixteen national boards of the Disciples of Christ report to the International Convention and their reports are included in the Year Book. The Convention office maintains a liaison relationship to all the organizations of the denomination.

The majority of Disciples churches and their members have always opposed the suggestion of a delegate convention; and, therefore, all members of Disciples churches who travel to the convention city and register for the assembly are allowed voting privileges. This makes for a mass assembly with preponderant numbers of registrations from the section of the country in which the convention city is located.

However, by providing the Committee on Recommendations, the International Convention has created a truly representative body within its mass assembly. The members of the Committee on Recommendations are appointed by the various state and provincial (in Canada) conventions. The local churches in these states and provinces, as they are represented in the conventions, have a voice in electing their members for the Committee on Recommendations.

All business of the Assembly of the International Convention, including reports, nominations and resolutions, is presented to the Assembly and immediately referred to the Committee on Recommendations. This Committee which has a total of 195 members is divided into several sections. Reports, resolutions and other business that are referred to the Committee are assigned to the sections, where thorough consideration is given to each matter and passed on with the recommendation of the section to the whole Committee. The recommendation of the Committee on Recommendations is then presented to the plenary body of the Assembly.

The Assembly can vote to approve the recommendation of the Committee on Recommendations or disapprove; or it can vote to refer the matter back to the Committee on Recommendations. Then, again, the recommendation of the Committee must come before the Assembly which, once more, can exercise one of the three aforementioned options.

Of all the agencies reporting to the International Convention the largest is the United Christian Missionary Society which is made up of: the Division of Home Missions, the Division of World Missions, the Division of Christian Education, and the Division of Central Departments.

Within the Division of Home Missions and Christian Education are the Departments of Church Development and Evangelism, Social Welfare, Institutional Missions, Religious Education and Missionary Education. The Division of World Missions administers the work of the Disciples in eleven countries, and also attends to the recruiting and training of new missionaries. In the Division of Central Departments are the Departments of Resources, Christian Women's Fellowship, Men's Work, Audio-Visual Services and Headquarters Service.

The United Christian Missionary Society has a Board of Trustees, which is the executive board, consisting of twenty-two members; and the Board of Managers which is elected from each state and province on a proportionate basis.

In the fiscal year 1954-1955 the total receipts of the United Christian Missionary Society were $4,428,436. Two hundred and forty-five missionaries were serving on foreign mission fields and there were 6,325 baptisms within the year on foreign fields.

One of the most important recent developments in missionary policy of the Disciples of Christ under the United Christian Missionary Society has been the integration of our work in Japan and the Philippine Islands with the United Church of each of those countries. This is in line with the historic conviction of the Disciples of Christ concerning Christian unity, but it marks a great advance in policy in that for the first time the Disciples have identified themselves with churches that do not insist on the practice of immersion.

The Disciples of Christ publish one of the outstanding missionary journals in Protestantism. The name of this monthly magazine is *World Call*. It is managed by the World Call Publication Committee which reports to the International Convention. Six representatives of the various phases of the work of the United Christian Missionary Society are members of the Publication Committee. In addition, there is one representative each from the Council on Christian Unity, the Board of Church Extension, the Board of Higher Education and the National Benevolent Association. The purpose of *World Call* is to present the world mission of the church. It reports chiefly on the foreign and home mission work of the Disciples of Christ, but also gives coverage to the world mission of the ecumenical church.

Another agency that reports to the International Convention is the National Benevolent Association, which traces its beginning to 1886. At the present time the National Benevolent Association administers seven homes for children and nine for the aged. In its history it has cared for approximately 25,000 persons in these homes. Nearly 1,400 are served annually.

The Christian Board of Publication, located in St. Louis, is one of the most important integral agencies of the Disciples of Christ. The charter under which it operates was granted by the State of Missouri in April 1911. Its purchase and early expansion were made possible by gifts from the late R. A. Long of Kansas City, totaling more than $404,000.

The charter provided that after necessary additions to plant and equipment, all profits accruing from the operation of the Christian Board of Publication must be used to advance the missionary, educational and benevolent institutions of the brotherhood. During the forty-five years of its existence up to December 31, 1956, the Board has distributed to these institutions $1,109,834. As of the same date the capital and surplus were $2,125,982.

Mr. Long said that the Christian Board of Publication was the most satisfying of all his church undertakings. Reference has been made to his gift of $1,000,000 to the Men and Millions Movement of the Disciples of Christ. He had a large part in the Emergency Millions program and in the building of the National City Christian Church in Washington, D. C.

Three laymen, noted for their philanthropies and extraordinary qualities of leadership, have served as president of the Board of Trustees of the Christian Board of Publication. The first was Mr. Long. The second was the late Palmer Clarkson of St. Louis. And the third was the late Oreon E. Scott, also of St. Louis.

After the death of Mr. Scott in January 1956 the executive head of the Christian Board of Publication, Dr. Wilbur Cramblet under whose direction the Board has had phenomenal growth, was given the title of President instead of Business Manager which he had held, and an able young layman, John McGinty of St. Louis, was named Chairman of the Board of Trustees.

It is sometimes said that the *Christian-Evangelist*, the weekly journal of the Disciples of Christ, is the "tap root" of the Christian Board of Publication. Long before the Board received its charter, the *Christian-Evangelist* was edited and published as a single enterprise. Printed now in color on one of the giant offset presses of the Board and having the largest circulation in its history, this journal is published at a loss of between $60,000 and $70,000 a year. The Christian Board of Publication absorbs this loss as an indispensable service to Disciple churches in the United States and Canada.

The Department of Church School Literature produces the Bethany Graded Series of Curriculum for each age group, the Bethany Uniform Lesson Series and a growing list of Bethany Elective Study Courses.

The Bethany Press is a department of the Christian Board of Publication. Books of general interest bear this imprint rather than that of the Christian Board of Publication. The Bethany Press has taken its place along with the other major denominational presses. The Christian Board of Publication, including its Bethany Press, is a charter member of the Protestant Church-Owned Publishers' Association, representing thirty-seven Protestant denominations and about 42,000,000 Protestant church members.

The Christian Board shares fully in the development of special curriculum materials produced under the direction of the Cooperative Publication Association for all Protestant publishing houses.

The Christian Board of Publication is interrelated with many other agencies and services of the Disciples of Christ. It acts as distributor for all sales material prepared by the several departments of the United Christian Missionary Society and other agencies. The Christian Board is a member of the Curriculum and Program Council that includes also, from the United Christian Missionary Society, the Department of Religious Education, the Department of Missionary Education and the Department of Social Welfare. This Council meets twice a year in order to integrate into curriculum published by the Christian Board of Publication, missionary and social welfare lesson materials. There is a close working relationship between the editorial staff of the Christian Board of Publication and the staff of the Department of Religious Education of the United Christian Missionary Society.

The Christian Board of Publication underwrites the budget of the Commission on Christian Literature of the Disciples of Christ. This commission promotes the reading of Christian literature by providing book lists for the churches, basic lists for their libraries and exhibits of books for Christian Literature Week.

Through its merchandising department the Christian Board of Publication gives another important service to the churches by making available communion equipment, Bibles, religious pictures, church records and many other needed supplies.

Other agencies reporting to the International Convention are: the Board of Church Extension, the Board of Higher Education, the Pension Fund of the Disciples of Christ and still others, totaling twenty-two.

A congregational system of church government has not only the problem of coordinating the objectives and programs of autonomous local churches into the aims and strategy of the whole brotherhood or denomination, but also the problem of securing a voluntary cooperation among the various agencies that must plead their causes before the separate congregations.

"Unified Promotion" has been devised by the Disciples of Christ to meet the latter problem. Since 1934 five of the national boards of the Disciples of Christ, the state and provincial societies and most of our colleges and foundations have banded together under Unified Promotion to present their combined needs to the local churches. Unified Promotion reports to the International Convention. To a great extent the formerly highly competitive approach of these agencies to the local church for support has been eliminated.

In addition to Unified Promotion there has been set up a Commission on Budgets and Promotional Relationships which reviews the work and needs of each agency, and then determines the percentage of the total income received by Unified Promotion that shall be allotted to each.

The growing sense of togetherness has been further marked by the creation of the Council of Agencies. Membership in the Council is made up of representatives of all member-agencies or institutions affiliated with them. Membership in the Council of Agencies totals approximately eighty-five. The work of the Council consists in mutual planning of the total program for the Disciples of Christ in the United States and Canada, and in the cooperative carrying out of that program. The Council of Agencies meets every two years, and serves for program clearing in a way that is similar to the budget clearance that is provided by Unified Promotion.

It has seemed important to the writer for the purpose of this story of the Disciples of Christ to relate the foregoing facts about the Committee on Recommendations, Unified Promotion, the Commission on Budget and Promotional Relationships, and the Council of Agencies in order to show how the Disciples are trying to overcome the weaknesses of local church autonomy, and separate and autonomous agencies, while conserving the congregational character of church government.

The spirit of this development is portrayed by a statement of the purpose of Unified Promotion in the Year Book of the Disciples of Christ:

1. To inspire people regarding the total Christian enterprise.
2. To mobilize the total strength of our Brotherhood.
3. To eliminate both the fact and the spirit of competition in the promotional approach of the agencies to the churches.
4. To avoid overlapping of effort by the correlation of the facilities and personnel of the existing agencies.
5. To serve the local church through a stewardship program of education, the provision of stewardship plans and the preparation of stewardship materials.
6. To assist the local church in making available plans and materials for the enlistment of every member for the support of current expense and missionary budgets.

It is interesting to note in this connection that the request for this united procedure came from the churches themselves through a resolution passed by the International Convention in 1931.

Prominent in this trend of voluntary cooperation is the

development in importance of the office of State Secretary, and the organization of the National Association of State Secretaries. The object of the Association, as stated in its constitution is:

> "... to promote fellowship; to acquaint one another with the methods of work employed in the different states; to promote the efficiency of the work for which its members are responsible; to coordinate programs and plans of work for state missions; to assemble reports of work actually done through the state society; to present the same to the International Convention of the Disciples of Christ, in the religious press of the Brotherhood, and in these and other ways to bring upon the Brotherhood life the impact of the total work of state missions."

The National Association of State Secretaries meets annually to discuss problems of interest to their offices and their respective states. The influence and even the power of state secretaries among the Disciples of Christ has increased significantly in recent times. A state secretary in our congregational system of government has no authority to appoint ministers to local churches and he has no prerogative to sit in judgment on any local church; but as his office is developing, the state secretary actually is becoming the most authoritative voice among Disciples in many states.

In many, if not yet in most, instances, the average local church will seek the counsel of the state secretary before calling a minister. It is hardly conceivable that a local Disciple church that is in full fellowship with the national and state organizations would call a minister of whom the state secretary disapproves. The secretaries, it must be stated, are cautious in their advice to churches about calling ministers. Their caution is prompted by their sincere regard for the autonomy of the local church, and also by an understandable fear of criticism if they assume undue authority over the local congregation. But, because the state secretary is being asked more and more for counsel by the local church as they are selecting a new minister, fewer mistakes are made in this most important matter.

A Disciple church in a small town in Kansas would have saved itself embarrassment recently if it had asked the state secretary for credentials for the man whom they called to their pastorate. It seems that he appeared on the scene without advance notice and talked himself into the pastorate of the church.

He must have had ability for soon the church was packed for the services and the congregation found itself in a thriving condition. But one day the sheriff of the county came and arrested him. The FBI reported that his record shows he had been convicted twenty-six times on felony charges. The minister confessed to the sheriff that he had been in prison for most of the past twenty years. He is now in jail.

The International Convention and the National agencies look to the state secretaries to present their program and the total program of the Disciples of Christ both to state conventions and to local churches within their states.

In addition to the state secretary, the city secretary has come to occupy a position of importance for the Disciples of Christ in many metropolitan areas. Because he serves a smaller area, the city secretary has become the program leader and the chief spokesman for the Disciple Churches in cities where Disciple churches are strong enough to support such an executive. Smaller churches especially have come to look

to the city secretary for leadership. The city secretary is usually surrounded by a city Disciple Union, organized into
committees vested with responsibility for guiding the churches
in the locating and development of new churches, in planning
programs on missionary emphases to be carried out in local
churches, in setting up laboratory schools, in promoting cooperative Christian social action, and in stimulating the local
congregations to meet their financial goals for missionary
and benevolent work.

All of this indicates that the Disciples of Christ are modifying the extreme position of local church autonomy that they
have held in the past. The change has come gradually, and
perhaps the churches have not been aware that in initiating
or going along with it they were modifying traditional patterns
as drastically as they have. The development that has come
may prove to have a potential that will ultimately mean more
radical departures from the extreme congregationalism of the
past.

There are some Disciples who fear this evolution and believe it will destroy the values of our congregational government. Others of us feel that the change will safeguard the
true values of congregationalism while safeguarding our
churches from ecclesiastical and spiritual anarchy. The change
will protect the local church from many a serious mistake
which it would make if it were to exaggerate its independence
from all other churches.

It appears to this writer that from both left (considering
congregationally governed churches as being on the left) and
right (considering the episcopal type of churches as being on
the right) denominations are moving toward a center where
variations of the presbyterian system of church government
is being attempted.

The Congregational-Christian Church has been moving in this direction for a good many years by local churches voluntarily associating themselves in their Congregational Council, and agreeing to consult with one another on such matters as the calling of a minister. Now as the union of the Congregational-Christian Church with the Evangelical Reformed Church is about to be consummated, the new United Church of Christ in America will be strongly presbyterial in its government.

The Protestant Episcopal Church of the United States and the Methodist Church have been moving toward this center from their traditional position. Bishops have been surrendering much of their authority to the congregations, especially in the matter of appointing rectors and pastors to local churches. While the office of greatest authority within American Protestantism is still that of the Methodist bishop, local Methodist churches increasingly are claiming the right to name their own minister.

What this means to the future of church organization and to the pattern which the United church, if and when it comes, will adopt, only the future can disclose; but there are these indications that the presbyterial system with its measure of independence for every local church, and yet with its orderly and effective oversight of the local church, by presbytery, synod and general assembly, may be the prevailing pattern of the future church.

The organization of a local Disciple church follows long-established precedents. The official board of a local church is made up of elders, deacons and, increasingly, deaconesses. The elders are supposed to be leaders in and guardians over spiritual matters. However, most Disciples ministers, and congregations as well, will confess readily that it is not easy in a Disciple church—nor perhaps in any other church—to distinguish between the things that are essentially spiritual and those that are mundane. Therefore, in most Disciple churches the elders do not meet separately unless the minister calls them together to help him face a crisis either in his own relations with the church, or in some family in the church, or with the conduct of some officer or member of the church. In most Disciple churches, elders assist the minister at the Communion Table; this is about their only distinguishing service.

The Official Board of a Disciple church is usually organized into functional departments such as: the department of worship, the department of evangelism, the department of missions, the department of education, the department of finance and the department of property.

There is in every Disciple church, of course, a Board of Trustees, required by the laws of the several states and provinces to be the legal custodians of the property of the church and to act in all legal matters for the congregation. Usually the trustees act only as the agents of the Official Board and congregation, and do not initiate any actions of their own. There are exceptions to this, and the church that I now serve in New York City is one of the exceptions. As the Board of Trustees of this church through the years has interpreted the religious statutes of the State of New York, they themselves take the initiative and assume the authority, independent of the Official Board, on matters that have to do with the property of the church and the permanent funds of the church. On budgetary matters the final authority rests with the Board of Trustees, although much freedom is granted to the department of finance within the Official

Board for the actual financial operation of the church's program.

But the final authority in every Disciple church is the congregation. The Board of Trustees, elected by the congregation, refers its most important decisions as recommendations to the congregation. The Official Board of a Disciple church would not assume authority for calling a minister. The selection of a minister is generally assigned to a committee, either of the Official Board or of the congregation itself; and the committee, after due deliberation, presents its recommendation to a meeting of the congregation.

By the religious laws of the State of New York, the minister of any Protestant church is the presiding officer for the congregation. But in most Disciple churches in other states and provinces, the congregation usually elects a layman, most often the chairman of the Official Board, as president of the congregation.

Again we have to say, because of the autonomy of the local church, practices differ widely within our churches. In some churches, the organization is poorly put together and slovenly administered. In other churches, the organization is carefully set up and efficiently operated. Within recent years, local churches have been calling on state and national agencies more and more for counsel and actually assistance in the organization of their congregations. There has been a notable development in effective local church organizations within the last generation.

The responsibilities of the minister in a Disciple church is determined to some extent, in fact in a large measure, by the minister's own temperament, and also by the character and efficiency of the lay leadership of the church. For many years I was pastor of one of the largest and strongest churches of the Disciples of Christ, a church that is characterized by its extraordinary lay leadership. Many things that I would have to do in a church with lesser leadership I did not have to concern myself with there.

However, I used to say that my job in that church changed with election of a president of the Official Board. The reason for this was that every man who was called to that high office had his own particular strength, and there was no need of attempting to do what he would do as well or better than I. Each man in succession, while having his peculiar strength, would find himself less able than his predecessor to take care of other matters. At that point I would have to supplement his leadership.

There is a philosophy of leadership involved here that is just as relevant to a congregation of another denomination as it is to that of the Disciples, but I speak of it here because the organization of a Disciple church is more flexible than a congregation of many other denominations. This philosophy is that one of the functions of a minister is to develop lay leadership, not only to give lay people the jobs that he would otherwise have to do but to give them the opportunity of developing themselves in the work of the church. There is the further consideration that a wise minister when he asks strong men to do a job for their church will credit them with the wisdom and initiative to do that job without his having to advise them at every step. With this philosophy of leadership the minister can inspire able men to undertake important work for their church.

EIGHT

SOCIAL CONCERNS

THE MOTIF OF Christian unity runs through the history and life of the Disciples of Christ like the theme in a symphony. This main pattern of their thought comes out even in their social concerns. Alexander Campbell held the churches of the Disciples of Christ together while the Baptist Churches, the Methodist Church and the Presbyterian Church divided at the time of the Civil War. Campbell did not concede that slavery itself is wrong. He, like many others, found support for slavery in both the Old and New Testaments. The slave traffic, however, he condemned because of the cruel and inhuman way in which it was carried on. His main objection to the institution of slavery was its effect on the mind and character of the white slave-owners. For this reason he felt that slavery should be abolished and he gave his influence to several proposals for the gradual emancipation of slaves. His sincerity in this position was evident by his freeing of his own slaves.

Alexander Campbell's support of the Fugitive Slave Law

justifies the following appraisal by Professor Roland H. Bainton of the Divinity School of Yale University:

"He had a frightful dread of division in the churches. The Methodists, the Presbyterians, and the Baptists were splitting over the issue. He would take no position which would cause the Disciples also to divide. His church unity program, in other words, made him less sensitive to the claims of justice." [1]

Now, it seems to this writer, the Disciples of Christ are made more sensitive to the claims of justice because of their mission to witness to the unity of the church. They send their representatives to every ecumenical conference; and, thereby, subject themselves to the Christian social conscience of all the other denominations. This fellowship both informs and inspires. God is present, and communicates Himself more clearly when the churches are together in His name.

A consensus of the churches on any social issue arrived at by free exchange of opinion, and in the fellowship of prayer, strengthens the conviction of every participating church. When, because of this consensus, the churches speak with one voice, they can be assured that theirs approximates the voice of the Lord, or that what they have to say is all that the Lord has revealed to them. In considering this development of the Christian social conscience we see how the Disciples' concern for Christian unity affects their social concern.

In nearly every community where there is a church of the Disciples of Christ, the almost unfailing participation of that church and its minister in the local council of churches, involves the Disciples in all programs of Christian social action. Again, we see how their feeling for the unity of the church bears on their position in social matters.

[1] From an unpublished paper on "Alexander Campbell and the Social Order" read by the author at a convocation at Bethany College, 1956.

As the Disciples work with their Christian brethren in applying the gospel to far-reaching social problems their primary concern for the unity of the church is increased because they see how ineffective any church is when it works alone.

The churches of the Disciples of Christ are guided in their study of social questions by the Department of Social Welfare, within the Division of Home Missions of the United Christian Missionary Society. This department advocates that every local church have a committee to lead the congregation both in social study and social action. A "five-point minimum program" is suggested for every church. A Social Action News-Letter with a supplement dealing with "Washington News" is published by the department.

Resolutions which the Department of Social Welfare presents to the International Convention reflect clearly, I believe, the major social concerns of the Disciples of Christ. The preamble to the latest comprehensive resolution (a single resolution, dealing with nine social questions) shows that the Disciples think theologically about social matters:

> "Believing that God is the Sovereign of this world and that His will is revealed both in the redeeming love embodied in Jesus Christ and in the experience of judgment seen in history;
> "Believing, further, that it is God's will for man that he should learn to live in terms of love and mutual respect and helpfulness with his brother; thus making real the kingdom of heaven 'on earth as it is in Heaven,' and believing that war, injustice, crime, intolerance and immorality are evidences of man's rebellion against God and the refusal of men and nations to acknowledge his sovereignty;

"Believing, also, that such social evils as war, racial intolerance, poverty, and the liquor traffic with their resultant personal misery and social tragedy are not only symptoms of man's rebellion and sinfulness, but also that they themselves lead to the breakdown, stunting and debasing of personalities and the destruction of spiritual values and that therefore those of us who wish to respond to God's desire that we accept responsibility for our brother's welfare, and live with him in love must not only abjure evil personally, but must work to eliminate evil processes from the social order;

"And believing that when men gather together to work and worship in the name of Jesus Christ they thus become a part of the body of Christ—the Church—and that as they do so they have a special responsibility to witness to his spirit, going beyond their own practice and wishes to speak to one another and to the world at large of what they believe to be His will;

"BE IT RESOLVED: that the International Convention of the Disciples of Christ . . . :

"1. Reaffirm its conviction that as members of the body of Christ, we should speak forthrightly and specifically of the sins of men, reminding them of the judgment and love of God as revealed in Christ and calling them to repentence, confession, baptism and the service of their fellowmen and their society;

"2. Acknowledges that the church, desiring His kingdom 'to come on earth as it is in Heaven,'

must make its actions parallel its prayers and
that it must seek to build a Christian world
order in which all men and women have the
greatest possible opportunity for physical, men-
tal, moral, and spiritual development; and
acknowledges also that this requires church
members as citizens and as a body of believers
to relate their convictions in concrete and
meaningful ways to the political, economic and
social structures of society;

"3. Recognizing the ambiguity of human moral
decisions and social policies calls the churches
and their members prayerfully to consider and
actively to support, where their conscience
allows, the following specific pronouncements:

Concerning disarmament it was proposed that the Disciples
of Christ support the efforts of our government through the
United Nations to secure multilateral reduction of arma-
ments, with adequate inspection under international auspices
to insure compliance with agreements.

On the question of universal military service and training
the International Convention was asked to restate the Disciple position, expressed many times, as being opposed to any
permanent system of universal military service and training.

The United Nations Children's Fund (UNICEF) was high-
lighted among other United Nations activities because it
"has performed an heroic mission of mercy among millions
of children on behalf of all of us."

Under the heading Citizenship this resolution called on
churches of the Disciples of Christ to include in their educational program such activities as:

   (a) a first voter recognition service for all individuals reaching twenty-one years of age, and for naturalized citizens:

   (b) a voter participation program in which each citizen would be encouraged to register and vote;

   (c) a candidates' night in which those seeking political office would discuss the issues with church members;

   (d) a series of "Round Table" discussions of the issues so that Christians may be adequately informed;

   (e) denominational and interdenominational seminars dealing with social issues.

Taking up again the old fight on alcohol and narcotics this resolution struck out against the advertising of alcoholic beverages, lamenting that the people of our country are "influenced more and more by advertising slogans and less and less by Christian ethics in formulating attitudes..." The relation of alcohol to public safety was emphasized. Alcoholics Anonymous was praised. The Board of Higher Education of the Disciples of Christ was requested to consider the establishment in one of our colleges of a department to study the social and economic aspects of the alcohol problem in a manner similar to that employed by the Yale University Center of Alcoholic Studies in its research regarding the physiological and psychological aspects of the problem.

In the section on religion in our daily work local congregations were urged to initiate programs of discussion and study dealing with such matters as:

   (1) the "doctrine of vocation"

   (2) labor-management relations

   (3) the place of women in business and industry

(4) the implications for the individual's employment to be found in his beliefs about the alcohol trade, world peace and similar social issues.

In the paragraphs dealing with the church and social welfare the Disciples of Christ were asked to meet the challenge of changing times in the "Message of the Churches" of the National Conference on the Churches and Social Welfare which met in Cleveland, Ohio, November 1-4, 1955. Special attention was called to the fact that although the population of the United States has doubled in the last half-century, the number of persons past 65 has quadrupled. The need of a specialized ministry to these elderly people was stressed. The churches were called on to work with health and welfare agencies. The church's responsibility to young people seeking vocations was also emphasized.

The greatest challenge to the Christian conscience was in the part of the resolution heading "Removing Racial Barriers." Acknowledgment was made of progress in opening our colleges and universities to minority races. Our national agencies were commended for employment practices that disregard race. Members of our churches who live in communities where racial tensions are critical were called to a special task of reconciliation. They were asked specifically to exercise initiative in forming voluntary interracial groups to encourage compliance with the law against segregation. Churches were called on to examine the real estate practices of their communities and their members with a view to encouraging the development of interracial neighborhoods. And the hope was expressed that churches would encourage one another in the effort to achieve a "non-segregated church in a non-segregated society."

The final section of the resolution on Public Education re-affirmed the Protestant Christian position in this nation on the separation of church and state. Churches were called on to alert their communities to the necessity of preparing school facilities that will be equal to the tremendous growth in popu-lation. Attention was given to the threat of some states to abandon their public schools because of the Supreme Court's decision regarding segregation. "Since we believe in equality of opportunity for all children regardless of race, economic background, religious tradition or geographic distribution, we support the Supreme Court's decision outlawing discrimi-nation in the public schools. We protest all efforts to establish privately controlled schools designed to support enforced seg-regation and discrimination in our society."

Attention was called to the pressures that are exerted in many communities and states for aid to private and parochial schools. Our position that only public schools should receive public money was reaffirmed.

As to the place of religion in public schools the resolution took account of those who favor the teaching of religion in public schools, but asked the Disciples to support "the idea of treating the study of religion from an historical point of view as we do the study of any other phase of our culture. It should be accorded full recognition in the curriculum on the grounds that to omit it is to omit an integral part of our American tradition."

This comprehensive resolution was thoroughly debated in the Committee on Recommendations and was passed by the Assembly of the Convention by an impressive majority vote. Not all Disciples will be guided by these directives but it is fair to say that the principles set forth here indicate the social concerns of the Disciples of Christ.

NINE

THE DISCIPLES AND ECUMENICAL THEOLOGY

A VISITOR FROM any other church to a Disciples' church would be hard put after hearing the sermon to recall any statement that he could consider peculiar to the Disciples. Certainly if the Disciples' minister were preaching on the text, "God was in Christ," the visitor could conclude that the sermon might just have well been preached from his Presbyterian, or, as the case might be, his Lutheran or Methodist or Episcopal pulpit.

If the sermon were on the subject of Revelation, or Redemption, or the Cross, or the Resurrection, or the Life Everlasting it is not likely that the visitor, even if he were the unusual person who today is well-grounded in the Bible or in the habit of thinking theologically, would note much that he could mark as peculiar to the Disciples' pulpit.

If this visitor were not content to taste one sermon but returned for a succession of Sundays, he might conclude that the sermons were less obviously theological and doctrinal than those which he would hear from the pulpits of other denominations. And yet, if he happened to be visiting a Disciples' church in which the minister is a young man, especially one who has been trained in an undenominational seminary, he might find that the sermons were not less but more markedly theological than he would hear in other churches.

This is due to the law of the swing of the pendulum which at the present time is tempting some of our younger ministers to try to show that the Disciples are as capable of theological preaching as others. I do not mean to indicate that this is done merely for show. In the great majority of instances, I am convinced, it is done out of a deep conviction that the message of God acting in Jesus Christ to bring redemption to men must be presented in terms of Biblical theology.

From the very beginning of their movement, the Disciples have had a sound sense that the source of all that is to be learned about God's revelation in Christ is the New Testament. The fathers of the movement failed to appreciate the significance of the historic creeds of the church as a faithful effort to summarize Biblical faith. However, they were right in their contention that no Christian could stop his search for Christ at any historic creed but that he must get back to the New Testament itself.

They did not have the means of Biblical interpretation that have been made increasingly effective by devout Biblical scholars since that day. Furthermore, their assumption that the New Testament intended to give an organizational pattern to the church was naive and unjustified. But their primary contention that the truth of God revealed in Christ must be appropriated from the Bible itself is supported by the scholarship of today with its emphasis on Biblical theology.

The whole church has come into a new theological era, and now it is discovering a new theological climate in which the study of theology is an ecumenical pursuit. Because of this new climate the Disciples, who have not been as theologically minded as some but more ecumenically minded than most, are susceptible to the theological development of the time.

The inquiry that the Study Committee of the World Council of Churches is making now on the subject of "The Nature of Unity We Seek" is being followed and participated in with extraordinary interest by the Disciples of Christ. For more than a century the Disciples almost alone were concerned with the question of Christian unity. For nearly all the other denominations the question had only marginal interest, if any at all. The ecumenical movement itself up until the present time has not given serious thought to Christian unity. In fact, there are denominations now affiliated with both the National Council of the Churches of Christ in the U. S. A. and the World Council of Churches that are on record as being prepared to withdraw from membership in these Councils if the matter of unity is pressed.

It has taken these years of studying and working together in the Life and Work and Faith and Order movements and in the National and World Council of Churches to bring the member-denominations to a point where they are willing to study the question of Christian unity. Before this time it has not been on the agenda of studies.

Because the Disciples of Christ have been isolated in their study of Christian unity, their own earlier conclusions crystallized into dogmas about the Disciples' having restored the "ancient order of things" and found the pattern for the unity of the church. This in reality was a declaration that other denominations would have to confess the error of their way and join the "true church."

But this position has been untenable by those ministers and churches of the Disciples that have kept in fellowship with ministers and churches of other denominations. And now the members of our churches who make up the main body of the Disciples of Christ look forward eagerly to what the ecumenical mind is to disclose on the nature of the unity of the church.

Christian unity is by its nature a question that no one denomination, apart from other denominations, can resolve. It is only by fellowship with other denominations in worship, study and work that the essential unity of the church can be experienced. The unity of the church is not something that men can create. It was given to the church by our Lord.

Humility is a prerequisite to a real venture in Christian unity. In an ecumenical fellowship, such as the assemblies of the National and World Councils, humility often results from the observation of the faith and character of Christians from many denominations. It is in this fellowship that the most creative work for the unity of the church is going on.

The Roman Catholic Church has kept itself outside this area where this creative work is being done. The call of the Roman Church to its own members recently to pray for the unity of the church sounded unreal and hollow because that church will not have fellowship with other churches, and denies that the church exists outside its own body.

Certain Protestant denominations that we might mention hold themselves outside the area where the creative study of Christian unity is taking place. Because they remain beyond this fellowship they cannot be influenced as the rest of our churches are by the interaction that comes when Christians are together in one place and pray earnestly for the leading of the Holy Spirit.

No separate church, not even the Roman Catholic Church, can fail to observe what is happening in the ecumenical fellowship, but a mere observer who holds himself aloof cannot enter into the mind and heart of those who are working together. The most fatal thing that can happen to a separate body of Christians is to be cut off from the creative thought and life of the rest of the church by refusal to be a part of the larger fellowship in which the Holy Spirit operates with greatest vitality.

From this point no one of us can predict where our praying and working together are going to lead us in the understanding of the nature of the unity of the church, but we have already experienced a degree of unity in our ecumenical fellowship that makes us sure that we must look to ecumenical theology rather than to the doctrine of any particular church for this understanding.

In a similar way, as the actualities of ecumenical experience provide new insights into the nature of the church, an ecumenical theology of the church will be far more comprehensive than any particular church's doctrine of the church. The nature of the church cannot be understood fully outside the ecumenical fellowship. There can be no adequate theology of the church that is not an ecumenical theology.

In the larger fellowship of Christians it becomes apparent that neither the Pope nor the Catholic Church nor the Patriarchs of the Orthodox Church nor any of the Protestant denominations holds the key to the church and the kingdom of God.

To know ministers and members of many denominations within the ecumenical fellowship is to be sure that the Roman

Catholic Church is in error in interpreting the Caesarea Philippi conversations, recorded in the sixteenth chapter of Matthew, as meaning that Christ meant to say that Peter was to be the first Pope of the Church, and that he and those in his succession as vicars of Christ were to receive the keys of the Kingdom.

For more than thirty years, in ecumenical worship, discussion and cooperative endeavor, I have experienced the "mystery" to which the Apostle Paul bore witness with never-ending surprise and gratitude. This "mystery" had to do with the nature of the church. In it Jew and Gentile were together, with no dividing wall.

The Jewish-Christians in Jerusalem were convinced that one first had to be a Jew or accept Judaism and its rites before he could take the further step that would make him a Christian. But Paul by preaching to the Gentiles found that this was not so. He discovered that Gentiles could by-pass Judaism and by a simple act of faith in Christ become Christians. The proof of this was the fruits of the Spirit in their lives. The Ephesian letter (this writer believes that the evidence indicates that Paul was the author of the Ephesian letter) exults in this discovery.

What Paul learned in close association with Gentiles, namely, that the church is not a fellowship that can be prescribed by men but is given by God, is being learned all over again in the ecumenical movement. The theology of the church, therefore, is bound to be an ecumenical theology.

What the New Testament knows of the early church is what the disciples experienced when they gathered together in the name of Christ. The nature of the church as the New Testament unveils it is the result of this fellowship.

We can read about the church there but we, like the early

Christians, can never know what the church is until we experience in the actual life of Christians meeting, praying, and
working together, what the first century Christian experienced. Individuals apart from their fellow Christians cannot
know the fullness of life with God, because God has reserved
that knowledge for the church. Christians who limit their fellowship to one local church also limit their knowledge of God
and of the church itself. Christians who confine their association with other Christians to the churches of their own
denomination also imposed unnecessary boundaries on their
understanding of God and the church. Those who widen their
fellowship into the ecumenical church always make new dis-
coveries of God and the church.

In the ecumenical fellowship, it is being revealed to us
more and more that the church is truly the body of Christ in
which His Spirit dwells. This is knowledge arrived at em-
pirically, but even so there is no accounting for the church
except that God in His providence determined to give the
church as a beloved community to those who accept Christ
through faith. It is God's providence also that His Spirit—
the Spirit of Christ, the Holy Spirit—operates within the
church.

Since the nature of the church cannot be known fully short
of the ecumenical fellowship, the theology of the church must
be an ecumenical theology.

Ecumenical theology is required to interpret the sacrament
of the Lord's Supper in a way that will account for the coming
of the grace of God in forgiveness and renewed strength both
to those Christians who will receive it only as it is ministered
by a priest in the apostolic succession and to those who will
receive it from the hands of a lay elder of the church. In fact,
ecumenical theology of the sacrament of the Lord's Supper

must also take into account how grace comes to plain men
and women in Quaker Meeting without benefit of the physical elements of the Sacrament.

The task of ecumenical theology in regard to the nature of
the ministry of the church is implicit in the preceding paragraph. But there are other considerations also that bear upon
the validity of one kind of ordination as contrasted with
another. Is the power to influence the mind and move the
hearts of men by the preaching of the Gospel given to ministers in one succession and withheld from those of another?
Are those whose marriage is solemnized by one ministry of the
church married in the sight of God, while those whose marriage is performed by another order of the ministry considered not to be married? The Roman Catholic Church takes
this position; but since Protestant churches recognize that all
couples who are married by their respective church are married, ecumenical theology must undertake a more thorough-
going study of the nature of the ministry.

In a similar way ecumenical theology has a task laid out
plainly before it to interpret Christian baptism so as to recognize that Christians are born of the Spirit both when they are
born of little water (sprinkling) and of much water (immersion). This ecumenical theology of baptism must be arrived
at by theologians who have been immersed and theologians
who have been sprinkled pursuing the subject together. Both
must subject themselves to Biblical revelation and to Christian experience. Both must free themselves as far as possible
from presuppositions and prejudices as they seek together the
leading of the Spirit.

At this point the writer needs to consider that some readers
may think that he has gone far afield from the subject that
has been assigned to him: "Why I Am A Disciple of Christ."

May I say in self-defense, and with a bit of pride that I hope is justified, that one cannot write of the Disciples of Christ without becoming involved in ecumenical discussions?

It is not within the competence of this writer to produce a book on ecumenical theology. Furthermore, it is not within the compass of this book as conceived by the publisher to formulate a systematic ecumenical theology. We, therefore, need not attempt to bring into our view at this time other subjects that must be brought within the scope of ecumenical theology. The subjects that have been introduced here indicate, I believe, the reasons for the vigorous study of ecumenical theology.

There is one more matter that bears on this general subject which we should consider briefly here. It has to do with the theological seminary. It would seem that if theological study in the future is to be mainly an ecumenical study, denominational seminaries ought to give way to union or undenominational seminaries where scholars from many churches and several main streams of theological tradition are brought together.

Peter Ainslie, the Disciples' "Apostle of Christian Unity," whom I have quoted before, expressed himself more than thirty years ago as believing that denominational seminaries ought to pass out of existence.

I do not believe he was right in this judgment. Earlier I have said that our loyalty to our particular denomination is justified, and even essential, until that time when the whole denomination can give the richness of its thought and life to the united church. If that position is defensible the further assertion is justified that denominational seminaries in the present structure of Protestantism have an important and necessary function.

All first-rate denominational seminaries are now ecumenical in the sense that they study the writing of the great scholars of the whole church through the centuries. I know of no seminary that would confine itself to the writings of its own scholars. Furthermore, the professors in many, and I think most, denominational seminaries have taken at least a part of their graduate work in some outstanding undenominational seminary.

A denominational seminary is in a position to influence the thought of the churches of its own denomination to a greater extent than the undenominational seminary for the reason that a greater number of their students go into the pastorate of their churches. Therefore, an ecumenically minded faculty in a denominational seminary has the opportunity of influencing the life of the entire denomination. I know of two seminaries of the Disciples of Christ, and there may be more, that have departments of ecumenics. The existence of such a department within the seminary is sufficient evidence of the sympathy of the seminary with the ecumenical movement.

While defending the denominational seminary, I wish at the same time to express the gratitude which I believe is felt by the leaders of my own denomination for the great undenominational seminaries that have brought to their faculties the outstanding Christian scholars of our time. These scholars by their teaching and their writing are influencing the life of the churches of nearly all the major denominations.

TEN

A DENOMINATION THAT HOPES TO DIE

THE Disciples of Christ are unique in that they are a denomination that hopes to die. There is nothing morbid in this. The hope is cherished in the way that the true Christian hopes for life after death. The Disciples hope to die in order that they may live more fully in the universal church of the Lord Jesus Christ.

During much of their history they contemplated the ultimate unity when all existing denominations, by some mighty outpouring of the Spirit in a new Pentecost, would acknowledge their sectarianism as sin and dissolve themselves into a united body, patterned after the church of the New Testament.

This dream was not put to a critical test for a good many decades because the historic denominations were not giving any serious thought to the question of Christian unity. If they were aware of the Disciples' dream of a united church they thought of it as just that, and were willing for them to go on dreaming. But as these other denominations, under the in-

fluence of the ecumenical movement, have become convinced
of the essential unity of the church and the urgency of ex-
pressing that unity both theologically and structurally, the
Disciples have had to face the challenge of their thinking.

The dream of the Disciples, therefore, has given way to the
realities of a widespread concern on the part of many denominations for the unity of the church. These realities include not only the new interest in unity but the difficulties
that stand in the way of achieving it. A thorough-going appraisal of these difficulties indicates that the road to unity will
have to be traveled a step at a time. Therefore the Disciples
of Christ have ceased concentrating on the end of the road
and are looking at the ground their feet must tread.

Now, most of us see that the ultimate unity depends on
denominations that have the closest affinity getting together
first. In this way the number of denominations can be re-
duced gradually.

I must say that the majority of Disciples still resist references to them as a denomination. When, in candor, some of
us Disciple ministers in our pulpits speak of our church as a
denomination, there is usually someone in the congregation
who, after the service, criticizes us for doing it. This happened to me not long ago. After I had spoken of our "denomination" a woman whose family has been in the Disciple
movement for generations expressed her real sorrow for my
designating our church in this sectarian manner.

But, of course, we are a denomination and the refusal to
wear the label does not change the fact. We have all the
marks of a denomination. We have a separate existence from
every other denomination, just as every denomination is separate from the others. We say that we do not have any creed

but Christ. There is a bronze plaque on the front of our church in New York which says, for all passers-by to read:

> This church defends no doctrine but Christ,
> Preaches no gospel but love,
> Has no purpose but to serve.

But what we say about Christ conforms to an unwritten creed; and, in our preaching, we deal with many gospel themes.

Our local churches have a large measure of autonomy—many of us think too large—but they are bound together in common beliefs and practices, in organization and in services that make them a denomination. We have a World Convention, an International Convention, state and regional conventions. We have our institutions: United Christian Missionary Society, Christian Board of Publication, National Benevolent Association, Board of Higher Education, and others. We have "Unified Promotion" in which the majority of our agencies that depend on the missionary and benevolent offerings of our churches promote their causes and divide their receipts according to agreed-on percentages.

We are a denomination. Yet we are peculiar in that while being a denomination we are not happy in our status. This discontent and uneasiness goes back to the beginning of our history when the fathers of the movement made a bold attack on the sectarian spirit of their time. The persistence of our effort to stem the tide of denominationalism has been marked by the terms we have invented to take the place of the word "denomination." Through the decades of our history we have referred to our "brotherhood," "movement," and "communion" to keep from using the word "denomination."

Today, those among the Disciples who put up the strongest resistance to the denominational concept, are most likely to refer to our "movement." In 1948 a "Commission on Restudy of the Disciples of Christ" that had been working for fourteen years, made its report to our International Convention meeting in San Francisco. This Commission, appointed by the Convention, discussed in its report the chief differences of opinion that made for tension within the fellowship of the Disciples of Christ. Under the heading, "Denomination or Movement," the Commission made the following statements:

"It is agreed that in our inception we were a movement rather than a denomination; that historically we have endeavored to avoid denominational status; and that to be content with occupying a status alone among many denominations is to abandon our attempt to realize unsectarian Christianity.

"Some of us hold that we must therefore refuse to accept any denominational status, and rather seek to occupy nonpartisan and ultimate ground in all points of faith and order.

"Others hold that we are compelled by the existing order of Protestant denominationalism to be a denomination, while at the same time testifying against denominationalism and exploring all possibilities of finding common ground on which all Christians may stand.

"Still others, in the judgment of this commission few in number, hold that we have in the processes of history become a denomination, possessing peculiarities and identity in a manner similar to the denominations round about us."

The writer of this book has put himself on record as one who believes that we are a denomination. He does not believe that those who in this matter believe as he does, are "few in number." Yet he acknowledges gratefully that the characteristics of a "movement" have been and still are marks of the Disciples of Christ.

There is no doubt that the Campbells and the other early leaders held to the idea that an important "movement" had gotten under way. Surely it was a "movement" when it protested against the exclusiveness of the parent denomination. It was a "movement" when it called itself merely an association. It was a "movement" when it was in the Baptist churches. This, the Baptists found out to their dismay and consternation. It was a "movement" when the two streams—that of the Christians under Barton Stone and the Disciples under Alexander Campbell—came together in 1832.

It has continued to be a movement where it has borne its witness to the unity of the church by seeking an ever-enlarging fellowship. One must note, however, that the portion of our fellowship which has become most denominational in its characteristics has held most tenaciously to the designation, "movement." It is they who exclude from their membership all who will not conform to their view of doctrine and organization. It is they who, as far as their own churches are concerned, have stopped the movement toward Christian unity.

Unlike these who think of themselves as conservatives—conserving the tradition of the fathers—the more liberal Disciples have really conserved the spirit of the founders of our movement by showing that they, like the founders, are not bound by tradition. It is this latter group among the Disciples who have kept alive the "movement" of our church in behalf of Christian unity.

I have said that we are a denomination that hopes to die. But I must admit that some among us are like the people who talk a great deal about the glories of heaven and indicate that they are eager to go there but protect their health very carefully so as to postpone the journey as long as possible.

The late Charles F. McCartney, long-time Dean of Transylvania College and noted Greek scholar and wit, had a heart attack while conducting a college chapel service. After some weeks of convalescence at home he went to Florida and spent several months in regaining his strength. He had been back only a few days when he was asked to respond to a greeting at the annual alumni luncheon. He told us that he had to make a very important decision early in the winter: he had to decide whether to go to heaven or go to Florida. He decided to go to Florida. His decision, he said, reminded him of a congregation in the old South that used to sing lustily, "Come, Angel Band, Come." "If one puny angel had showed its head above the organ," he vowed, "the people would have fled out doors and windows."

Something like this mingling of desire and dread is felt by the Disciples as they contemplate their demise as a separate body of Christian people, but I believe that there is a very sincere hope on the part of the greater number of people that some day—and not too distant a day—our church will no longer exist as a distinct body but will be an indistinguishable part of a church in which several—we hope many—churches will have found their unity in Christ. The spirit of John the Baptist lives in the hearts of our people. We want to decrease in order that our Lord and His church may increase.

There does not seem to be any chance of ridding the Christian World of denominationalism except by the denominations growing in grace to the point where they are willing by action of their corporate bodies to lose themselves in a great whole. The relatively brief history of community churches indicates that this is true. Some of the most sincere advocates of Christian unity have gone into community churches in order to give effective witness to their convictions. The dilemma of community churches is that while standing against denominationalism they, almost inevitably, have to become a denomination in order to have fellowship with other like-minded congregations. Although they keep their assemblies as non-official and informal as possible these assemblies take on the characteristics of a denominational meeting as they consider what they as separate community churches should be doing together. Disciples, perhaps more than any other communion of Christian people, understand this dilemma of the community churches, for in many ways they are re-enacting our own efforts to keep from becoming a denomination.

Today, because of the historical development of denominationalism within Protestantism, that which is unique in any denomination is dependent for its witness upon the spirit, the strength and the persuasiveness of that particular denomination. The merit that there is in the Episcopal form of church government could not be presented effectively to the Christian world by individual Episcopalians and Methodists apart from their denominations. Whatever truth and merit there is in the doctrine of apostolic succession requires the witness of a denomination, like the Episcopal Church, that exemplifies the actual operation of this doctrine. In like manner, whatever the Lutherans or the Presbyterians have that they want the rest of the denominations to have, must be borne to the growing ecumenical fellowship by these denominations.

This points again to the intervening steps that have to be taken by the denominations before they achieve their ultimate comprehensive unity in Christ. Those denominations that have the most in common, should accomplish their own unity first. This has been done by the several separate bodies that now make up the Methodist Church. We would hope that the Presbyterian denominations could find the way to become one church in the not too distant future. It is not clear to some of us whether there is an affinity deeper than the common name that can bring Southern Baptist Churches and American Baptist Churches together. Lutheran denominations have an obligation not only to themselves but to the whole of Protestantism to find the road to their unity. Sooner or later the Episcopal Church and the Methodist Church should rediscover each other at a common point in their history and then move forward together.

The union of the Congregational-Christian Church and the Evangelical-Reformed Church which now seems certain to take place before this book is published, indicates that unions may take place on a broader base than we had formerly thought. It has been assumed that the three basic but different forms of church organization—congregational, episcopal and presbyterian—would be the rallying points for the earliest mergers of denominations, but the above-named union that is about to take place is bringing together a church that has a congregational form of government and a church that has a modified presbyterian form of government.

This supports an observation that we have made at another point in this writing to the effect that Protestant church administration seems to be shifting from a pure congregationalism on one side and an authoritarian episcopal government on the other side toward a kind of presbyterian pattern between the two. Therefore, we would predict that Christian unity will develop according to this pattern.

The Greenwich Conference on Church Union has called forth a widespread and, in some places, deep interest among the Disciples of Christ. In June 1946 at Grinnell, Iowa, the Congregational-Christian General Council in its biennial meeting passed unanimously a resolution requesting the Federal Council of the Churches of Christ to invite those denominations which "recognize one another's ministeries and sacraments" to send representatives to a conference to explore the possibility of a closer union.

In August of the same year the Disciples of Christ at their International Convention seconded this resolution, but suggested a more inclusive invitation to be addressed to "those communions which are in sufficient accord in essentials of Christian faith and order to give promise that such a conference would result in further and effectual achievement of Christian unity."

At that time there were twenty-four denominations that were affiliated with the Federal Council. The invitation was given to each of these. The following nine denominations accepted the invitation to participate in the proposed conference: Methodist, Presbyterian USA, Presbyterian US, Congregational, Christian, Disciples of Christ, African Methodist Episcopal, Colored Methodist Episcopal, and the Association of Community Churches. It was estimated that these bodies at that time represented about forty percent of American Protestantism.

The first meeting of the appointed representatives took place at Greenwich, Connecticut, in December 1949. Since then this body has been known as the Greenwich Conference on Church Union although it designated itself simply as the Conference on Church Union. At this intial conference it was unanimously agreed that they should seek for nothing less than "an organic union" of their several bodies, "a fellowship and organization of the church which will enable it to act as one body under Jesus Christ who is the Head of the Church."

The writer has been told that there is disappointment that the nine denominations that responded to the original invitation have not taken more seriously the studies of the Conference, but this disappointment can hardly relate to the Disciples of Christ. At the International Convention of the Disciples of Christ held in Des Moines, Iowa, in September 1956, three breakfast meetings that considered the work of the Conference up to date drew capacity attendance. After several meetings of the Conference a Drafting Committee had drawn up "A Plan For a United Church in the United States" which was "Proposed for study by the Greenwich Conference on Church Union." It was this initial and tentative "Plan" which the Disciples had before them at the breakfast meetings.

Before the Des Moines Convention, over a period of several months, Disciples groups in many sections of the country had been meeting to consider the "Plan." My information is that no other denomination has taken the studies of the Conference with anything like this seriousness.

At this stage of the development of the "Plan" it would not seem advisable to report it in detail in a book, and I doubt if the officers of the Conference would give us the permission to do so. However, "The Common Faith" which the Conference has affirmed for the participating denominations is significant and can be recorded:

"We Are One in common faith of the Christian Church and in our desire to share as a common heritage the various historic and treasured expressions of that faith.

"We Are One in common belief
    in God our Father;
    in Jesus Christ, his only Son, our Savior;
    in the Holy Spirit, our Guide and Comforter;

in the Holy Catholic Church, through which God's
eternal purpose of salvation is proclaimed and his
Kingdom comes on earth;

in the Scriptures of the Old and New Testaments as
disclosing the Word of God for men, from which
new light is evermore breaking forth for us and
for our world;

in the forgiveness of sins;

and in the life everlasting.

"We Are One in our faith that the Church is of God and
in the deepening sense of obligation with which we hear the
prayer of our Lord for his disciples, 'That they may all be
one; even as thou, Father, art in me, and I in thee, that they
also may be in us, so that the world may believe that thou hast
sent me.'

"We Are One in that spirit of love which, owning the same
Lord, recognizes diversity of gifts, concerns and ministrations,
and assures to all freedom in ways of worship, and of witness.

"We Are One in our purpose that this United Church of
Christ be dedicated to our Lord for the furtherance of his redemptive work in the world."

Since the spirit in which The Conference on Church Union
(Greenwich Conference) is proceeding in its study appears to
the writer to be the spirit that must characterize all adven-
tures in Christian unity we quote a paragraph from the
"Study" that reflects clearly this spirit:

"The United Church of Christ is predicated upon mutual
respect and appreciation of the precious traditions in thought
and practice which each participating body brings to the
union. It is committed to spiritual freedom. It does not desire
conformity in practice of uniformity in thought except as our

fellowship in work and prayer draws us closer to each other. We believe, however, that the fullest measure of organic union presupposes an ever-widening degree of common polity, common forms and materials of worship, and common ways of thought. As we grow in oneness of heart and mind, it seems inevitable that we would appropriate more of each other's traditions and, beyond any of those traditions, develop new traditions of worship and polity which would express our spiritual unity. It is suggested, therefore, that with the establishment of the United Church of Christ, some commission on study and appraisal be appointed, adequately representing our various traditions, to review the progress of the union, to encourage steps toward achieving higher levels of oneness in life and work and worship, and to propose such practical instruments of common life as a hymnal, a book of worship, orderly forms of ecclesiastical procedure and the like."

If all or the majority of the denominations that formally associated themselves with the Greenwich Conference were to proceed in this spirit to plan and work for a united church, the Disciples of Christ, I believe, would show an ever increasing interest in it. But because most of the other denominations seem to have cooled toward the Conference it seems to this writer that we can be more optimistic about another possible union.

ELEVEN

UNITED CHURCH OF CHRIST

THE HEADING of this chapter is the name that has been chosen for the church that will come into being by the merger of the Congregational Christian Churches and the Evangelical and Reformed Church. The new church will be a reality before this book is published.

The writer is sure that a brief discussion of the United Church of Christ is integral to this story of the Disciples of Christ. During the last fifteen to eighteen years while the Disciples have continued to talk about their historic "plea" for the unity of the church, the Congregational Christian Churches and the Evangelical and Reformed Church have worked through many problems and frustrations toward the union on which they had set their hearts. Opponents of the union within the Congregational Christian Churches even resorted to the courts in their attempt to defeat the negotiations.

The initial skepticism about the union of churches as different in organization, historical background and doctrinal emphasis as the Congregational Christian Churches and the

121

Evangelical and Reformed Church, was hard to overcome. I knew something about the first conversations out of which the dream of this union took form. I was pastor of the Union Avenue Christian Church in St. Louis when Dr. Truman Douglas, then minister of the Pilgrim Congregational Church, just across the street, and Dr. Samuel Press, then president of Eden Theological Seminary in suburban Webster Groves, began to say to one another that it was clear their churches ought to unite.

The Disciples of Christ at their International Convention in Buffalo, New York, in August 1947 passed a resolution, written by me, that shows their peculiar interest in the proposed union. That we were too sanguine about the time that is required for the negotiation of such a union is evident in the wording of the resolution:

"Whereas, the proposed union of the Evangelical and Reformed and the Congregational Christian Churches will likely be consummated within the next two or three years; and since this union, when it is realized will bring together four historic communions of diverse history, doctrinal emphases, and ecclesiastical polity, manifesting that there can be unity in diversity; and

"Whereas, some of the leaders of these uniting churches have openly expressed their hope that this body of unity would continue to grow, and have further stated that they look to the communion of the Disciples of Christ as the next fellowship of Christians with whom they should discuss the possibility of forming this united church; and

"Whereas, the historic passion of the Disciples of Christ has been the increasing union of the church;

"Be It Resolved, that the International Convention of the Disciples of Christ, meeting in Buffalo, New York, in the summer of 1947, authorize the Association for the Promotion of Christian Unity to explore the possibilities of our sharing in this growing body of unity."

The Association for the Promotion of Christian Unity changed its name a few years ago to the Council on Christian Unity. The Council proposed to the International Convention, meeting in Des Moines, Iowa, in September 1956, that it reaffirm the resolution of 1947 because of the assurance that the Union of the Congregational Christian Churches and the Evangelical and Reformed Church would be consummated in June 1957.

The resolution was reaffirmed by a unanimous vote of the convention. Since then many leaders of both the uniting denominations have expressed their pleasure at the action, and scores of Disciples have inquired when negotiations would get under way.

Of course, the Disciples will wait for an invitation to enter into discussions from the United Church of Christ. We do not expect this invitation to come in the near future because we know that the merging denominations face an enormous labor in consolidating their new position. But I have no doubt that the invitation will come and I am equally sure that the great majority of Disciple Churches, including both their ministers and members, will wish their representatives to pursue discussions and negotiations with the earnest hope of bringing the Disciples into the United Church of Christ.

At this point it must be understood that the writer is speaking only for himself. There would be no need to say this if he were not president of the Council on Christian Unity and some people might assume that he is speaking for that organization. But I believe I am reflecting the mood of the Disciples of Christ generally when I say that we shall take up the challenge of the United Church of Christ with a deep seriousness.

If they were to back away from this challenge they would

sacrifice the right to continue their historic witness for the
unity of the church. That they would not have to sacrifice
any of their convictions in order to be in the United Church
of Christ appears evident from a close scrutiny of the Basis of
Union drawn up by the Congregational Christian Churches
and the Evangelical and Reformed Church.

Surely the Disciples of Christ could affirm the Faith to
which the merging denominations witness in their Basis of
Union:

"The faith which unites us and to which we bear witness is
that faith in God which the Scriptures of the Old and New Testaments set forth, which the ancient Church expressed in the ecumenical creeds, to which our own spiritual fathers gave utterance
in the evangelical confessions of the Reformation, and which we
are in duty bound to express in the words of our time as God
Himself gives us light. In all our expressions of that faith we seek
to preserve unity of heart and spirit with those who have gone
before us as well as those who now labor with us.

"In token of that faith we unite in the following confession
as embodying those things most surely believed and taught
among us:

"We believe in God the Father Almighty, Creator and Sus-
tainer of heaven and earth and in Jesus Christ, His Son, our
Lord and Saviour, who for us and our salvation lived and died
and rose again and lives for evermore; and in the Holy Spirit,
who takes of the things of Christ and shows them to us, renewing,
comforting, and inspiring the souls of men.

"We acknowledge one holy catholic Church, the innumerable
company of those who, in every age and nation, are united by the
Holy Spirit to God in Christ, are one body in Christ, and have
communion with Him and with one another.

"We acknowledge as part of this universal fellowship all
throughout the world who profess this faith in Jesus Christ and
follow Him as Lord and Saviour.

"We hold the Church to be established for calling men to

repentance and faith, for the public worship of God, for the confession of His name by word and deed, for the administration of the sacraments, for witnessing to the saving grace of God in Christ, for the upbuilding of the saints, and for the universal propagation of the Gospel; and in the power of the love of God in Christ we labor for the progress of knowledge, the promotion of justice, the reign of peace, and the realization of human brotherhood.

"Depending, as did our fathers, upon the continued guidance of the Holy Spirit to lead us into all truth, we work and pray for the consummation of the Kingdom of God; and we look with faith for the triumph of righteousness and for the life everlasting."

It is not conceivable that the name of the new church could be a stumbling block to the Disciples. In some areas our church is known as the Church of Christ. However, there is confusion among us about the name. The churches that broke with our fellowship over the question of instrumental music and formed a separate communion adopted this name. And, adding to the confusion, the fundamentalist churches that have more recently withdrawn from the cooperative life of our brotherhood have chosen to designate their churches by the name, Church of Christ.

The merging congregations, in a footnote to the Basis of Union, have taken into account a difficulty that they may encounter with this name. The Disciples of Christ will testify that this difficulty is very real because they had a similar difficulty in trying to hold to the simple name, Christian Church. "If the name 'United Church of Christ' seems presumptuous," says the footnote, "it should be remembered that any good general name must seem so, since it would apply equally well to other groups. A name, however, quickly becomes a mere means of classification, and it is hoped that the world will soon come to know that the Churches uniting under this name do not pretend to be more than they actually are."

We have discussed in an earlier chapter the problem that the name has been to our church. I think I can say without being successfully contradicted by those who know our history that the reason our churches in recent decades have been more and more hesitant about referring to themselves as the Christian Church, and have come generally to refer to our brotherhood as the Disciples of Christ, is that the rest of the Christian world made us feel that we were "presumptuous" in the use of this name. Perhaps we should not have been so timid before this charge of presumption. Anyway, as we have already reported, the recent assembly changed the name of our convention to the "International Convention of the Christian Church (Disciples of Christ)."

The name "United Church of Christ," I believe, would please our people.

The Disciples of Christ will find themselves in full agreement with the first paragraph of the section on "Practice" in the Basis of Union: "The basic unit of organization of the United Church of Christ is the Congregation; that is, the local church."

The second paragraph indicates how the organization is to develop from this "basic unit": "The Congregations, through their ministers and through delegates elected from their membership, may organize Associations for fellowship, mutual encouragement, inspiration, and such other functions as may be desired."

The next paragraph continues with this emphasis on the Congregations: "The Congregations, through their ministers and through delegates elected from their membership, constitute Conferences for fellowship, counsel, and cooperation in all matters of common concerns. The Conferences exist to make cooperation effective (a) among their Congregations and (b) between their Congregations and the General Synod, the Board, commissions, agencies, and instrumentalities of the Church."

From this point the Basis of Union moves beyond the congregational autonomy that Disciple churches have held for themselves: "The Conferences, through delegates elected by them from the membership and ministers of the Congregations located within their respective bounds, constitute the General Synod. . . . The government of the United Church is exercised through Congregations, Associations, Conferences, and the General Synod in such wise that the autonomy of each is respected in its own sphere, each having its own rights and responsibilities. This Basis of Union defines those rights and responsibilities in principle, and the constitution which will be drafted after the consummation of the union shall further define them but shall in no wise abridge the rights now enjoyed by Congregations."

It must be assumed that since the General Synod of the United Church of Christ will be a delegated body and "shall carry on the general work of the Church which is now conducted by the General Council of the Congregational Christian Churches and the General Synod of the Evangelical and Reformed Church" that it will have an authority which the congregations of the Disciples of Christ have never granted to their International Convention. However, with the safeguards that the Basis of Union is giving to the congregations some of us among the Disciples of Christ would be pleased with the orderly and responsible procedures that are implied in this kind of church government.

The spirit with which it is anticipated that the congregations of the United Church of Christ will work together

within the framework of this organization is revealed in the
paragraph that deals with the calling of ministers.

"The calling of a minister to a Congregation is a concern
of the Church at large, represented in the Association or
Conference, as well as of the minister and the Congregation.
Ministers and churches desiring to maintain a system of pastoral placement in which the Conference or Association shall
have little or no part, shall be free to do so; but the recom-
mended standard of denominational procedure shall be one
in which the minister, Congregation, and the Conference or
Association cooperate, the Conference or Association approv-
ing candidates, the Congregation extending and the minister
accepting the call. The new communion will appeal to all
Congregations not to call or dismiss their ministers, and to
all ministers not to respond to calls or resign, until the Association or Conference shall have given approval. In all relationships between minister and local church or Congregation,
the freedom of the minister and the autonomy of the church
are presupposed."

The Disciples of Christ who have suffered and been many
times embarrassed because congregations have acted inde-
pendently and without counsel in the calling of ministers
should approve of this provision which leaves the ultimate decision with the congregation and yet recognizes that the whole
church has a rightful concern about every minister-congrega-
tion relationship.

When the time comes for the Disciples of Christ to be
brought into conversation with the United Church of Christ
the question of baptism is certain to be the most difficult that
will have to be faced. Disciples, as we have emphasized in the
earlier part of this book, hold to the conviction that baptism
is a believer's rite. This is their primary concern in any dis-

cussion about baptism. They believe that they have a witness about this matter which must not be lost.

Immersion as the apostolic form of baptism has great significance for us. The fact that Jesus was immersed and that the Apostle Paul came to see in baptism by immersion the symbol of the death and resurrection of Jesus Christ, and also the symbol of the Christian experience of dying with Christ that we might live with Him—all of this gives baptism a rich association that we feel we cannot lose.

It appears, however, from the emphasis on local church autonomy in the Basis of Union that there is ample room within the United Church of Christ for congregations that would bear this witness.

One cannot predict what modifications of present doctrines and practices would result from the leading of the Holy Spirit were the Disciples of Christ to become merged with the United Church of Christ, but he would expect the Disciple members of this union to come to a deeper understanding of the meaning of infant baptism. This would not mean that they would surrender their convictions about believer's baptism but that they would invest the dedication of babies with much of the significance that infant baptism holds for the other members of the United Church of Christ.

The solidarity of the Christian family is demonstrated when parents present their newborn child to the church for baptism. This act indicates that the mother and father think of their child as born not only into their home but also into their church. The element of dedication is inherent in infant baptism. Some parents look upon the rite as solely one of dedication. But although the infant cannot take any initiative in his baptism there is a sense in which he does ask for it, a sense in which he does witness to his own belief, a sense in which he does confess his sin and seek forgiveness.

The parents act for the infant, but there is this profound sense in which the infant, still with no language but a cry, acts through his parents. God has set the solidarity in families. From the hour of his birth the child is given the hands and feet, the mind and voice, the aspirations and faith of his parents. He moves about and expresses himself through them. He goes where they go. He says what they say. We know that these acts, of which he is not conscious at the time, become a part of him. For good or ill, his whole career of consciousness will have to reckon with this earliest self. Fortunate is the infant who can express himself through Christian parents.

The service of dedication of babies as practiced by the Disciples of Christ would be enriched by appropriating much, if not all, of the meaning attached to infant baptism. If this were to happen, the service of dedication would, conceivably, take on an importance that would bear significantly on any restudy of baptism in the United Church of Christ, or anywhere within the ecumenical movement.

No great difficulty is anticipated over the Disciples' insistence on the weekly observance of the Communion of the Lord's Supper if, and when, we enter into negotiations with the United Church of Christ. Where a Disciple congregation would become identified with the United Church it would be expected that the Communion would continue to be celebrated as an integral part of every Sunday morning service. Where former Disciples would be in a church that had belonged either to the Congregational Christian Churches or the Evangelical and Reformed Church there could be a Communion Service at an earlier, or later, hour in the sanctuary or in a chapel.

We ought not to be concerned about the full amalgamation of members of formerly distinct denominations in the United Church of Christ. The Spirit will be there in greater power because all these disciples of our Lord are together. Under the Spirit's leading, more and more of God's Will will be opened to them, and they in turn will become more and more one body and one spirit.

The Disciples of Christ have talked a great deal about their willingness to die in order to increase the unity of the church. The Congregational and Christian Churches and the Evangelical and Reformed Church have laid down their lives for the United Church of Christ.

What will the Disciples of Christ do?

TWELVE

WHY I REMAIN A DISCIPLE
UNTIL . . .

MORE IMPORTANT than why one became a member
of the church of the Disciples of Christ is why he remains
a Disciple. I suppose, as I have indicated in the early pages
of this book, that I became a Disciple for the same reasons
that other persons became Methodists, or Presbyterians, or
Episcopalians.

One of my parents was a Disciple and it was almost inevitable that I would go into the church of one or the other
of my parents. Perhaps one might remain in the church of
his childhood because of inertia or apathy. I think that
would not be true in my case because I have had an ever
deeper interest in religious matters, and certainly I have a
more critical judgment of the church than I had when I became a member of a Disciples' congregation.

My great interest in the ecumenical movement has caused
me to attend the services of many churches of other denominations. I also have studied their history, doctrines, organization and practices with the result that I have a deep, and

I believe an informed, appreciation for all the major denominations. However, I must confess that I have never been tempted to leave my denomination and seek membership in any other. I pray for the time when the Disciples of Christ in a body will unite with another denomination, or with several denominations that will merge into one large united church. I am hopeful that before I die the Disciples of Christ will cease to exist as a separate communion. But until that time, I am convinced that no other church can satisfy my own religious needs as well or give me, as a minister, a better opportunity to preach the gospel as I understand it than the Disciples of Christ.

Much of this feeling, I am sure, is due to the fact that my roots are deep in the Disciple movement. Some of it, I am equally sure, is caused by my involvement as a minister in the organization and program of our brotherhood. But after I have faced frankly these facts, I am still certain that until the day of the consummation of the witness of the Disciples of Christ, when they lose themselves in the larger Body of Christ, no other denomination could meet my spiritual needs as well or satisfy my ministerial hopes better.

I hasten to say what has certainly been evident in previous chapters, that I am not uncritical of the Disciples of Christ. I lament that while we have talked a great deal about Christian unity we have not exemplified that unity in our own history. Many of our churches have carried the principle of local church autonomy to indefensible extremes. I have been disappointed in many of our ministers and churches whose backward look to the founders has betrayed the founders themselves, for they were men who were not bound by tradition. The literalism in Biblical interpretation that has characterized some of our ministers and laymen has made for division which has belied our witness for the unity of the church. We could go on and list other faults and sins of the Disciples of Christ. But in face of all of these, I am still happy to be a Disciple.

The Disciples of Christ, it seems to me, are the least inbred of the major denominations. Therefore, we can appropriate for ourselves truth from whatever source it comes. The fact that we do not have an historic creed does not cut us off from history and tradition, but rather allows us to adopt whatever commends itself to us as true and significant. The Disciples are free to view all historic traditions objectively. This is a tremendous advantage now when the ecumenical spirit prompts many churches to share their historic treasures with one another.

I have my moments of grace when I am not jealous of the longer history and the greater prestige of certain other denominations which saves some of us Disciple ministers from the too great self-assurance and pompousness that we seem to detect once in a while in some other quarters.

On the level of city councils of churches, I have noted, sometimes with regret and sometimes with chagrin, the spirit of self-sufficiency on the part of the representatives of some of the older and stronger denominations that kept them from being as helpful as they should be in the cooperative work of the churches. For instance, I have witnessed these more powerful denominations refusing to cooperate in teacher-training programs because they were abundantly able to provide teacher-training schools for their own teachers. I have seen them stand aloof from union services which would have brought inspiration to whole communities because they could fill their own churches with their own members.

The Disciples have not been altogether guiltless in these

matters because there are places in this country where our churches are very strong. In many towns and cities of the midwest, the churches of the Disciples of Christ are predominant in strength and influence. However, their historic sense of mission to bear witness to Christian unity usually influences the minister and members of even the strongest Disciple church to associate themselves with all interdenominational programs.

I am happy in the Disciples' church because it is not a class church. The cultured and the plain folk, the rich and the poor, the older families and many without deep roots in the community make up the average congregation of the Disciples of Christ.

A church does not need to discourage the rich from coming into its membership in order to demonstrate its democracy. Rich people need the church as much as the poor. And certainly the church needs the support of rich people. Most of the wealthier Christians that I know want above all else to be appreciated as persons and not for their wealth. Most of them reject any preferential treatment.

We can understand why some rich people are suspicious of the motives of ministers and churches that show an undue interest in them. In the church and out, they are cultivated too often for the favors they are in a position to grant.

While the Disciples of Christ cannot be rated with the wealthier denominations, we have always had in our membership some people of large wealth. Some of these have been true stewards of the possessions in their hands. I am informed that the first Christian layman in this country to give a million dollars to his church was a Disciple. I refer to the late R. A. Long who in the second decade of this century gave a million dollars to the Men and Millions Movement of the

Disciples of Christ. This was not his only large gift to the brotherhood. He purchased and presented to the church our publishing house, the Christian Board of Publication. He made also a generous gift to our National City Christian Church in Washington.

I am pleased to be a minister of the church of the Disciples of Christ because I am convinced that my church, to a greater degree than most, allows me a free pulpit. Certainly I do not imply that I have an irresponsible pulpit. While the non-creedal position of our church makes us heirs to all the creeds, and places us in the full stream of church history from the New Testament days to the present, for the same reason we are subject to the restraint of all the truth into which the Holy Spirit has led the churches through the centuries.

Often I have been impressed with this when I have heard ministers of other denominations proclaim dogmatically the creedal positions of their own churches as though their church alone were custodian of the whole truth. Therefore, although I feel that I have the freest of pulpits, I am also aware of the restraint of having to take into account that which is precious in the eyes of other Christians and other churches.

But the freedom of the pulpit which is so important to me is the freedom to speak without fear of ecclesiastical authority. I am free to proclaim from my pulpit the truth that has impressed itself on my mind and heart. Of course, if I were to violate that freedom by careless pronouncements that ran counter to the basic truth of the Gospel or completely contrary to the main body of Disciple tradition, I would have to reckon with the ultimate authority of a Disciples' Church, the congregation itself.

Where the belief in the priesthood of all believers prevails, the people have the right and the obligation to engage their minister in religious discussion. The lay mind is important in the dialogue not because the lay mind is a theological mind but more especially because at times there is revealed to the lay mind that which is hidden from the theologically wise and understanding. The Gospel that I preach from the pulpit has been confirmed for me innumerable times in the developing faith and character of those to whom I preach.

The questions and doubts of these lay people have been of as great significance to my preaching as their affirmations of faith, for these queries and proddings have driven me back to my study and, often, to my knees in search for answers and a simpler wording of the truth.

Encounter with earnest laymen is the surest way of keeping the minister humble. Only as he is humble will he be teachable. Although Disciple ministers ordinarily do not turn their backs to their congregation and face the cross in the chancel when they lead in public prayer, as ministers of the more liturgical churches habitually do, thereby identifying themselves with the worshipping congregation, we, in both our praying and our preaching, are aware that we are in exactly the same relation to the cross and to God as those to whom we minister. This identity of pastor and people has been impressed on me often when, after giving a message that I myself needed, I discovered that it had more than usual significance to members of the congregation.

The congregation carries an added weight of responsibility in its relation to the pulpit because the minister alone cannot achieve this mutuality. If preaching should be a dialogue between pulpit and pew—and I insist it should—the members of the church ought to be reading and studying the Bible along with the minister. I am sorry to report that not a great many members of the Disciples' church appear to be doing this. The preaching dialogue between preacher and congregation in many instances is almost broken down because the people do not understand the minister's Bible references. Whereas, for instance, a simple reference to the vision of Peter as he was about to receive messengers from Cornelius should call forth a clear picture in every Christian's mind, the average minister now knows that he must take the time in his brief sermon to retell and explain that story. Before the preaching in Disciples' pulpits—and I suppose we could say the same about other Protestant pulpits—can achieve its ultimate power, the congregations must again begin to read and study their Bibles.

The freedom that is allowed a Disciple minister as a leader of worship enables him to draw upon the vast storehouse of worship materials that belong to the church universal. And yet he can, and is expected to, bring into the service prayers and litanies of his own composition. Perhaps the majority of Disciple ministers never write their pastoral prayers. Some, I am afraid, do not prepare them at all. But an increasing number of our ministers, especially the younger men, are giving great care to their preparation of services of worship.

Dr. G. Edwin Osborn, Professor of Practical Theology of the Bible College of Phillips University at Enid, Oklahoma, has edited for the Disciples of Christ a volume entitled *Christian Worship, A Service Book*. This book has unusual merit because it includes a comprehensive manual of worship and a large collection of prayers from many sources. The publication of this worship book by the Bethany Press is an indication of the greater attention that is being given to worship forms on the part of the Disciples of Christ.

The Disciples have published two outstanding hymnals in recent years, indicating again the ever higher standard of worship materials they have set for their churches. The Bethany Press has published the hymnal, *Christian Worship,* edited by a joint committee representing the American Baptists and the Disciples of Christ. The Baptists also have published this hymnal under their own imprint. The Christian Foundation of Columbus, Indiana, has published an excellent hymnal edited by Mrs. Clementine Miller Tangeman. Both of these hymnals rank with the best hymnal in Protestantism today.

As I consider why I am happy to remain a Disciple I must refer to two features of the Sunday morning service of worship in every Disciples church of which I have already written at some length. The weekly observance of the Communion of the Lord's Supper is so integral a part of the Sunday morning service of worship that most members of our churches feel keenly the lack of it when they attend a service in a church of another denomination. We have discussed the dangers that are inherent in this frequent observance, such as the tendency of people to neglect their preparation for it and even participate in it thoughtlessly. But after all these possibilities have been admitted we must say that the greater number of Disciples think of the Communion as the climactic part of every Sunday morning worship service.

Another feature of the worship service in a Disciples' church is the reception of new members. Following the sermon in every service the minister gives the invitation to membership in the church and then a hymn of invitation is sung, during which the persons desiring membership come forward to be received by the minister.

For a service to close without this invitation seems to me to show a lack of confidence in the persuasive power of the proclamation of the gospel. Furthermore, it seems to me to be very unfortunate for persons who may have experienced in the service a desire to become members of the church to be given no invitation to do so then and there.

This leads me to write of another reason why I have maintained my loyalty to the Disciples of Christ. The Disciples are, and always have been, an evangelistic people. In the early days they broke through a theological fatalism and persuaded hundreds and thousands of people that they could become in the truest sense of the word children of God by the simple profession of faith in Jesus Christ. They were told that they could rest their faith upon the evidence in the New Testament that "God was in Christ."

In times past, the evangelistic zeal of the Disciples expressed itself most characteristically in revival meetings. Evangelists were invited into the local church about once a year to hold a two or three weeks revival meeting. In the mid-west they were called "protracted meetings."

In more recent times the revival meeting has given way, entirely in many places, to the continuous program of visitation evangelism. The members of the group meet regularly to study and discuss methods for making their witness more effective. At these meetings they are given cards with the names and addresses of the prospects on which they are to call. They "covenant" with God and with one another to be diligent in their efforts to win these people to Christ and the church. The vitality of most Disciple churches can be determined by the faithfulness and zeal with which the continuing program of evangelism is carried on.

Still another reason why I am happy in the ministry of the Disciples of Christ is that most of our churches are characterized by a warmth of fellowship. Strangely, the intimacy and depth of this fellowship seems to increase with the size of the community where the church is located. This does not mean that rural and village people are less friendly than the people in metropolitan cities. It does mean that the church means more in fellowship to its members in a vast, impersonal city than it does in a small community where every one knows every one else and people see each other in all the phases of the community's life. In the big city the church is the community to its members, and it is the only real community that they experience. Because of the informality of its worship and the democratic composition of its membership, the Disciple Church is well adapted to answer the people's need for fellowship. It would be hard to get in and out of the average Disciple church on any Sunday without receiving a cordial greeting from a number of people.

I am sure that most of the characteristics of Disciple churches which I have mentioned are shared by the churches of other denominations but because I find them in our churches I am content to remain in the ministry of the Disciples of Christ until that time, for which I pray, when the whole body of Disciples will first die and then come into a more abundant life by entering into unity with another body of Christians.

INDEX